# Through Nature's Lens:

## Do We Really Love Our Land and Water

Neil D. Hamilton

Ice Cube Press, LLC (Est. 1991)
North Liberty, IA, USA

*Through Nature's Lens: Do We Really Love Our Land and Water*

Copyright ©2025 Neil D. Hamilton

ISBN 9781948509695

Library of Congress Control Number: 2025xxxxxx

Ice Cube Press, LLC (Est. 1991)
1180 Hauer Drive, North Liberty, Iowa 52317
www.icecubepress.com  steve@icecubepress.com
Check us out on Facebook, Bluesky, and Substack.

The paper used in this publication meets the minimum requirements of the American National Standard for Information Sciences—Permanence of Paper for Printed Library Materials, ANSI Z39.48-1992.

Made with recycled paper.

Manufactured in Canada

Photo credits: All photos provided or taken by author.

Disclaimer—It should go without saying, but the opinions, views, and comments in this book are solely those of the author and nature. They should not be ascribed to any other organization, institution, or individual with whom he may have contact. If you have complaints, take them up with the management! Of course compliments and kind words are always welcomed.

Praise for Through Nature's Lens

"How fortunate we are to have Neil Hamilton's illuminating perspective on what we must focus on as crucial issues today for our children and grandchildren. We are all intrinsically connected to each other and this planet. Our actions, or lack of action, have significant repercussions. With his expertise, knowledge, and wisdom, Professor Hamilton weaves a compelling and creative montage of the urgent steps we must take today for a healthy and balanced future."
—Jan Lovell, Iowa Natural Heritage Foundation, Board member

"Many great thinkers such as Henry David Thoreau and Aldo Leopold have shaped our collective philosophy on the natural world and human interaction. Hamilton – a great thinker of our time – moves these grand ideas into reality. He forces the conversations surrounding how the 'rubber hits the road.' If we believe in conservation and the right of nature to exist for its own sake, THEN WE MUST do something about it! He asserts that all aspects of our current world paradigm, including commodity agriculture, politics, education, and public health must be examined. No one aspect gets a free pass. Hamilton's prose convey the haunting reality of the current state of our natural world, balanced with an optimistic plea for action. This is a must read for people who are concerned, but are perhaps uninformed, and want a roadmap to action."
—Rich Leopold, Director, Polk County Conservation

"As a cancer doctor, I take great interest in the health of each and every one of my patients. By extension, I'm also very interested in the health of our planet. These interests are inextricably connected. What happens to our planet, happens to us. We are facing a cancer epidemic in Iowa. This is caused, in part, by the way in which we are assaulting our land and rivers with a toxic mix of chemicals and run-off. *Through Nature's Lens* is a wise and compelling guide to the role that nature plays in our lives. It's also an alarm bell to wake us from our slumber of complacency."
—Richard L. Deming, MD, FACR, FACRO, Medical Director, MercyOne Richard Deming Cancer Center

"Neil Hamiton issues a bracing call for us all to recognize and assume our civic and environmental responsibilities. Deploying his great breadth of knowledge and decades of personal and professional experience, he points us toward a future in which our ethical relationships to the land and to one another are honored and, most important, acted upon."
—Curt Meine, author, *The Essential Aldo Leopold: Quotations and Commentaries* and *We Can Do Better* the collected writings of Paul Johnson

"Through personal reflection, insightful stories, and hard-hitting facts, Neil Hamilton explores our relationship with Nature. While his focus is on Iowa and on agriculture, his message is for all to hear. And he pulls no punches—degraded waterways, climate change, and the 2024 Presidential election. What does Nature have to say about it all? Where can we find hope for the future? Once again, Hamilton has produced a book that everyone should read."
—Professor Susan A. Schneider (she/her/hers), William H. Enfield Professor of Law, Director, LL.M. Program in Agricultural & Food Law, University of Arkansas School of Law

"I echo Neil's speaking for Nature: 'one spot of good news in all this is the comfort, relief, and joy I provided so many of you. The soothing evening hike, the weekend at the beach, the fishing trip to the lake, nature (me!) has been able to and will continue to provide the comfort to ease your minds and soothe your souls.'"
—Mike Delaney, Racoon River Watershed Association board member

"A personable and persuasive exploration of the natural world's many voices. *Through Nature's Lens* first challenges us to accept that nature's future is indeed our own, and then gifts us with straight-forward responses for redirecting our lives and Earth's future. Hamilton's best book yet!"
—Cornelia F Mutel, author/editor of 7 books on Iowa's natural environment

"In *The Land Remains* and *The River Knows*, Neil Hamilton gave voice to the Back 40, a field on his childhood farm, and the beleaguered Raccoon River. Now in *Through Nature's Lens* he gives Nature itself a voice that deserves to be heard throughout the Midwest. Hamilton's open-hearted, insightful, and all-too-timely book holds great significance for Iowa's natural landforms and for their advocates and appreciators. People who may not realize how much they rely on the comfort and beauty of nature will have cause to thank him in the future."
—Holly Carver, former director, University of Iowa Press

"Nature may prove to be the most eloquent of the powerful voices Professor Neil Hamilton has captured in his compelling trilogy: *The Land Remains, The River Knows* and now, *Through Nature's Lens*. Nature's perspectives come from below—ground up, sky down, through crosswinds, deep roots and creatures—invasive through endangered. The Professor's work compels us 'to consider another player' as we come to understand the challenges we face with our current ag system and our failure to act. Yet, forever the optimist, Neil and his nature friends offer 'hope and new big ideas to embrace.' Ignore them at our collective peril. This is a must-read."
—Pat Boddy, former deputy and interim director of the Iowa Department of Natural Resources, and senior partner emeritus of RDG Planning and Design in Des Moines

"Neil Hamilton has been a central figure in efforts to prevent the decimation of Iowa's natural environment after decades of unrestrained and unregulated activity from the industrial agriculture sector. His new book takes stock of where we are in this fight a quarter of the way through the 21st Century as viewed through the eyes of nature. This book is ideal for anyone desiring that the most fertile agricultural region in the world can someday contribute to an environmental and public health renaissance rather than being a symbol of environmental degradation and biodiversity loss."
—Adam Shriver, Director of Wellness and Nutrition Policy, Harkin Institute for Public Policy and Citizen Engagement

"Hamilton has spent a career as a sleuth, problem solver, and visionary. While his focus has been in agricultural law, his passion for truth telling always drives his take on farming, ranching, and rural development far beyond the field, feedlot, orchard, and small town. In *Through Nature's Lens*, he completes his trilogy engaging the foundations of agriculture by inviting the reader into a dialogue with the land, water, and now nature. He takes often complicated issues of law and policy and makes them comprehensible, familiar, and accessible for everyone with an interest in a deeper appreciation for how we can all live better together on Earth."

—Matt Russell is a 5th generation Iowa farmer, USDA appointee in both the Obama and Biden administrations, and an agricultural leader for over 25 years at Catholic Rural Life; The Drake University Agricultural Law Center; Iowa Faith and Climate Network, and Iowa Farmers Union

"Neil Hamilton is the nation's preeminent author on agriculture, land, and water law. His new book on nature is a 'must read.'"
—Sarah Vogel, Attorney and author of *The Farmer's Lawyer*

*Dedicated to the*

Public school teachers educating children,
opening minds to truth and knowledge;

Librarians safeguarding storehouses of
culture against bigotry and intolerance;

Government employees protecting nature,
enhancing our quality of life; and

Lawyers committed to justice, insuring
the rule of law remains paramount.

The fate of democracy depends on your confronting the
forces of ignorance, hatred, and greed now threatening
our nation. Our future and nature's future depend on you.

# THROUGH NATURE'S LENS

# Chapter 1
# Who Speaks for Nature?
# An Introduction

If nature could talk to us, what might it say?

Would we like the answers?

Would we appreciate its perspective?

Would we change our ways if it asks us to or told us we need to?

Could it be, nature is talking to us already but we aren't listening? Are we even able to hear or recognize its voice, among all the other noise and distractions of modern life? Or do we expect nature to speak to us in human terms, in a language we understand and if we aren't hearing anything, then all must be fine?

Nature *is* speaking to us, trying to get our attention in more natural ways. Nature's messages are carried on the wind, in the dry scorching heat driving droughts and feeding California wildfires. Its messages are there in the torrential downpours sweeping the Gulf Coast, flooding the Appalachians and the Northeast, and playing havoc with our lives. Of course this is not how we like to think or to see things. These are just meteorological events, shifts in weather patterns, yes, probably influenced by climate change and human actions, but still just that. We find satisfaction in our mechanistic explanations and science-based understandings of what is happening or, for some in their faith, whatever that might mean to them. Either way, we don't have to contemplate the idea these events might be messages from nature or nature's way of speaking in the only language it knows.

There is comfort in our way of thinking. We don't have to raise our vision above ourselves, to consider another player. One with autonomy, needs, and influence in this game of life. It is proving hard enough to manage our own human actions and motivations without adding more worries. Why complicate things by thinking there is more involved, more to consider, so we don't. To us nature is simply the canvas on which we paint our lives. We hope and believe nature is benign, a neutral player, perhaps even a benevolent friend looking out for us. We believe nature needs us to protect and save it, not the other way around. This is a soothing way to view the natural world, a predictably human perspective, but the question remains: Is it true?

The land has a story and the water has one, too—these I tried to capture in my books *The Land Remains* and *The River Knows*. The truth is we all have our own stories to tell, and I encourage you to put yours down in writing if for no other reason than to share with your family. The key story for this book is that of nature. This is my effort to tell at least some of its story, one you'll hear in part through nature's voice. Why am I qualified to do so, you ask? There are a number of reasons: my long career as a professor of agricultural law, my work with various land organizations and other personal involvements—you can look at my bio if this is important to you. You could ask the same questions about my qualifications for writing about land and water. The main reason for telling their stories is because I choose to. The main reason to write these books is because there are important stories to be told and to be heard, lessons to be learned, and exciting questions to ponder. Plus they are fun and engaging to write and even more satisfying to share with readers like you.

I chose to write this book because nature has its own important story to tell. No one can decide who is not qualified to tell nature's story. I trust you to judge whether what you read is of interest or value. I want to tell the story of nature because it is so encompassing. We exist in the world of nature and only because of it. Certainly the land is a major part, in many ways the stage on which nature performs. Water is another essential player, critical to existence and central to the shape of society and our economy. Nature has many other components—the air we breathe, the wildlife and other living things, plants and animals, birds, insects, and fungi comprising the living world—these are parts of nature. So too are the minerals we mine, the energy sources we rely on to heat our homes, fuel our cars, and sustain our existence. The weather, collectively the climate, is part of nature, as are the landscapes themselves. Whether mountain ranges, prairie grasslands, desert valleys, or scenic coastlines—all lands are part of the nature where we live.

Viewed this way, nature is a very large cake, one perhaps impossible to grasp or eat in one book. Fear not, that is not my goal in writing about nature. This story, our story, is told through the lens of nature. It concerns the parts we commonly encounter: the farm fields, rivers and lakes, prairies and grasslands, forest and timbers, and wildlife populating them, these are our subjects, as well as trails, parks, and wilderness. In other words, the subject is the nature we use, enjoy, and rely on every day of our existence.

Why choose this more limited view of nature? Because these are the parts we know best and have thought about the longest. This is the nature underpinning our lives, producing our food, filling our time, and offering enjoyment, restoration, and inspiration. It is the nature we most intimately and immediately affect. We shape its health with our choices, actions, attitudes, and policies. We can benefit by increasing our understanding of its needs and ways. In this regard, our interactions with nature provide the context and opportunity for hearing from nature. To listen to it, reflect on how it experiences our care or lack thereof, regards our respect or abuse. As we will see, these forces and attitudes combine into a rich stew of love and contradiction, reflecting how we deal with nature. So here we are, ready to set off together on another adventure in bookmaking. When we get to the end, I hope you will have found it rewarding, interesting, perhaps humorous and at times upsetting, but never dull.

Why another book? What is there left to say? These are questions any author needs to answer—and answers you deserve to hear. The question came to me on a research trip to New York City in April 2024, standing in the Strand bookstore, surrounded by thousands of books on shelves seeming to stretch for miles. If you love bookstores, a visit to the Strand is worth a trip to the Big Apple. There are so many books it seems like everyone living must have written one. That is when the question hit me—Do people need another book from me?

As you realize, my answer was yes—you are holding it. But let me share more reasons why this book exists. Most important, I have more to say, more insights to offer, more truths to reveal, and more rocks to turn over in a quest to understand our relation to nature. Certainly the land and river books, which I hope you have read or soon will, tell a great deal of the story, offering history, humor, and hope. The main goal for writing is the opportunity it gives us to think as I had to. My main lesson from writing about the land and river is readers are hungry for information, interested in challenging accepted wisdom, and thirsty for creative ways to think about and then act on our relation to the natural world. Using the Back 40 and the Raccoon River to help narrate the stories of the land and water broadened the voices and helped us recognize the community we share with the natural world. That is why this installment is told through the lens and voice of nature. Many familiar elements will appear—land, water, history, farming, food, and the role of law. In many ways the book is woven with themes of nature and our search for justice, the warp and weft of nature's cloth—what it means to us, how we use it and abuse it, and what it needs as we shape a future for ourselves, our children, communities, and state living with nature.

Stories about individuals working across the broad face of nature provide both inspiration and context for our exploration. My experiences, drawn from over 40 years of teaching about the law and the land, provide reflections and insights on how our desire for justice moves us forward and about the distance we still need to travel. The goal, as Aldo Leopold knew, of learning to live on a piece of land without destroying it is still beyond our grasp, but we are making progress. Even with the challenges we face—extreme and radical political shifts, an antiregulatory mindset coupled with ever growing demands on nature, and an uncertain climate—there are many reasons for hope and new big ideas to embrace. This is why I wrote the book and why I hope you will find it worth your time to read.

## Nature as the Narrator

Greetings, Nature speaking. If you have read the professor's books on the land and the river, you've been expecting me, wondering when I was going to make an appearance. Well, here I am, right on cue. First, a note on what to call me. I am very aware people commonly speak of me fondly in gendered terms as Mother Nature. This is the image Ding Darling, one of my most creative and eloquent advocates, used in the wonderful drawing pictured here. He masterfully captured both the ages I spent storing up the inventory of what you label natural resources and the profligacy with which many of your kind are burning through them. So if you feel the need, I am okay being seen as a mother figure, a nurturing, caring soul concerned with your needs and future. On the other hand, if you want to think of me as a masculine power, especially when my weather rages with tumultuous impacts, that is fine as well. Perhaps I'm neither male or female, or possibly I'm both, but then your new political regime seems to want to make that illegal—so much for respecting nature's designs.

*Time To Take An Inventory of Our Pantry*

Either way, you should know I don't necessarily see my work, and all I am about, in such a gendered way or as benign as the image Mother Nature may suggest. Nature is powerful, as your weather and my geology can attest. Nature is autonomous, independent, and in many ways devoid of feelings or concerns for your needs. Sorry to break it to you, but I was here first and can get along just fine without you. But we both know that is not possible—you are here now so we must coexist if we are to thrive. Unfortunately I am vulnerable, subject to the actions and uses of those who live on and through me. Cutting down my forests, eroding my soils, channeling my rivers, these are all actions or insults I can do little to stop, at least in the near term. This is why I need friends, people who know me and care for me—the nature lovers if you will, the Leopoldians, the good stewards, all those who care about me and think about how their actions affect my future and my feelings. This is why I am honored to add my voice and share my insights where they might be helpful as the professor tells this story—the tale of how his life has been refined and refracted as seen through nature's lens—my eyes.

The journey takes us back to the formation of your nation and sweeps forward to headlines from today. It involves traveling to towns and places across the state, meeting friends of nature new and old, and discussing social trends and activities of everyday life. Some of the stories are told by looking to nature and connections to the professor's life. Now I have to admit at this stage that while I agreed to be tasked as a willing narrator, I am not sure this linkage will bear the weight of the story he hopes to tell. All I can say is, for both our sakes—you as the reader and I as the narrator—let's hope he can make it work!

## THINKING ABOUT NATURE AND ITS FUTURE

As the calendar turned to the first quarter of our new century it seemed a good time to take stock of where we are in our relationship to nature and the resources so important to us in Iowa and across the Midwest. This helps explain the reason for completing this final part of my nature trilogy. The first part, *The Land Remains,* was published in spring 2022, while the second part, *The River Knows,* was published in summer 2023. My hope is you are reading this by late 2025. As you can tell from the title, our focus is nature—where we are, where we are headed, and how we can find hope in our relationship with the natural world. The book doesn't follow a formula, but builds on the writing from before. You will find a combination of lessons drawn from history; personal experiences and observations from my years teaching about agriculture, law, and conservation; discussion of current developments in our state bringing into sharp focus our relations to nature; and critical insights into where we are and where we are headed. Because I am writing in the first half of 2025, the unfolding chaos and havoc being leveled by the new administration, much of it on nature and its friends, require attention as well.

My working title for this book was originally *The Road to Hamilton,* the idea being a memoir built on personal experiences and looking for connections to people, products, and places bearing my family name. While that may sound like an interesting concept, if your name is Hamilton, even I recognized it was a bit too self-absorbed and asked too much from readers. Thankfully for both of us, I regained my senses and the focus returned to my original idea for a nature book, one told using the lens of justice, something I have worked to promote.

Even though I have spent my life as an academic, teaching students, lawyers, and citizens about the role of law, my perspective here is not to approach issues academically, but instead to describe them in terms and stories we can all appreciate. I refer to this as putting the corn down where we all can eat. First though, I must ask for a moment's grace to set out some thoughts that may seem more academic. Please bear with me for a few pages as I build a structure for how we can consider the relationship between nature and culture, helpful when considering the various issues to be addressed.

## WHO OWNS NATURE?

To examine the question of nature's future, we must start by asking a different question—who owns nature? There appear to be three choices: individuals, society (the public), or no one. We can eliminate the third option simply by looking around. We can see that most of nature, in many ways comprised primarily of land, is owned by someone, mostly private but with some public. (Of course, nature may have a different reaction on this point, knowing very well no one owns it, but for now let us stick with how we humans see the matter.) The land contains or is made up of much of what we think of as nature—the land, the trees, and wildlife—even the scenery. One exception may be the water found in our lakes and rivers. We often live next to it, with our houses on the edges, and we recreate there, but for the most part water is owned by the public. Even so, private acts clearly affect water quality—is it safe to drink and are what lives in it, such as the fish, healthy? Even resources we don't think of as being privately owned, for example, the air we breathe or the views we see out the window as we drive, can be affected by the actions of others. Air can be polluted and views can change with developments—as billboards go up, trees are cut down, and buildings are constructed. So the answer to who owns nature is someone else—that is, except for the parts you may claim your ownership to. Why ask this question then? Because the answer helps explain what factors shape and determine the health of nature as we experience it and, more importantly, will influence its future.

We can think about our relationship to nature and its relationship to us by considering five primary forces shaping how we interact: culture, justice, democracy, freedom, and the economy. All help define how we experience nature and how it will shape our future. Let me explain these five forces and their relationship to nature as represented by land, water, and wildlife, in otherwords, the stage on which we lead our lives.

Culture is represented by society and human relations. The events and details of our lives are largely shaped by our cultural existence, including powerful forces like religion.

Justice is represented by fairness, equity, and respect for others, raising questions of where and how justice happens

Democracy is represented by government and politics, in how collective decisions are made and how individuals relate to others within the system.

Freedom, what you may think of as liberty, is represented by our individual rights to function in society, in culture, and in relation to others. This includes concepts of private property and owning nature, such as land.

Economy is represented by the structure where decisions and activities take place, for example, how we earn a living and how society pays for services. In many ways the economy reflects the range of our available life choices.

First, culture affects how we see nature. Think about your culture or that of any actor. We may all be Iowans, but we have different cultural ideas and expectations. One reason to think about culture is because it does several things—it can explain our starting point, how our ideas of nature and our relationship to it were formed. It can introduce or identify what may need to change (if possible) if we want different behavior. For example, there is a powerful cultural dimension to private property, with many expectations about what we believe ownership to mean. These reasons help explain our natural resistance to regulations or restraints on land use, as well as our lack of acceptance of common land ownership. The point being that U.S. culture is for the most part individualistic as opposed to what might be a more collective culture.

Thinking about cultural norms and the cultural dimension for our nature actions is valuable in understanding why we do what we do. As we will read in chapter 4, much is written about water quality in Iowa and the impact current agricultural practices have. Acknowledging that farmers' actions flow from and are supported by powerful cultural forces can take some of the blame off individuals as bad actors and instead, ask if agrarian culture and farming systems need to change.

Our farming culture, discussed in chapter 4, is almost entirely yield oriented, the cultural value centered on productivity. People promoting soil conservation have struggled against this reality for decades. Viewed in this light, the question shifts to what might it take to influence or change our culture? You might argue an increased awareness of the dangers to human health, is a possible starting point for problems to be examined. This idea certainly underpins many efforts to understand and address Iowa's surprising ranking as having the second highest cancer incidence in the nation, a subject we examine in chapter 3. When confronted with new information about how certain practices, such as widespread use of pesticides, may be connected, the reaction of some might be "I've never looked at it like that" or "I didn't know that was the effect." Of course others, especially those in agriculture, see any suggested connection between pesticides and cancer as an unwelcome attack. A second opportunity created by discussing potential causes is to identify alternatives to present practices, to reduce the risks of making changes. What does it mean to be successful or respected? Is it big yields and a well tended farmstead? Could it instead be fertile fields, thriving nature, and healthier people? What does the culture value?

Another dimension of the culture and nature connection involves the type of nature in which a culture develops. Consider the difference between individuals living in a cold Arctic environment where nature may seem brutal and harsh and those residing in a more moderate climate were nature is fruitful and giving. The modern extension of this geographical connection between nature and culture is how the natural world where you grew up or live affects your views. If your background was an Iowa farm there was probably little nature or diversity near you or much wildlife. This undoubtedly affects your thinking about nature, its potential, and what might be reasonable to expect. Think of the number of times you have heard someone say "here in Iowa we don't have mountains or oceans or forests but we do have"— leaving you to fill in the blanks with some local attraction. Your exposure to nature may influence your later views about its importance to culture. I grew up on a small farm in Adams County where trees were relatively few and far between, yet my connection to nature was fueled by travels to western parks and was solidified when I attended forestry school at Iowa State University. The importance of early exposure to nature is what makes examining nature-based education projects a key theme, as discussed in chapter 8.

The culture and nature connection has implications for the other primary forces, for example, what is our culture for justice? Do we expect it, and are we offended by injustice? The relation of justice to nature has shaped much of my career and is the focus of chapter 9. Our culture is clearly a democracy with citizens given the opportunity to influence government actions locally and nationally. Typically we are offended by nondemocratic actions, such as presidents usurping powers to act like kings and state officials granting eminent domain power to a private company to take farmland. A force related to democracy yet more individual is the idea of freedom, also seen as liberty. The nature-culture equation considers how freedom relates to individual and community relations. Our society places great value on individual autonomy and the idea we are responsible for our decisions and any success we experience. Yet we all live embedded in layers of community, in an economy that creates shared responsibilities and social expectations.

Let us hear what our narrator may think about this process.

## How Nature Sees Its Cultural Context

Thank you, Professor, for asking for my input on your attempt to put my relationships into some form of larger cultural context. Here is how I see the elements you have listed.

I see culture as the ways in which society engages with and enjoys me.

I see justice as the processes used to protect me from abuse and to resolve conflicts between differing views of what I mean for individuals and society.

I see democracy as the political process whereby social priorities are established and my autonomy and identity are recognized and respected.

I see your freedom as a potential threat, as a lack of restraints on individuals, unless society recognizes my right to exist.

I see the economy as how and why individuals consume or use various parts of me—as how I am harnessed to deliver the financial benefits used to support your society's existence. Clearly producing food, harvesting timber, and all the ways you obtain energy are part of how you use nature.

Finally, I believe there is another force, really a sixth element you need to add to your equation, one leading to the rest of our story. This is the future. We all have a history and we all live in the present, but by thinking about our actions and possible threats to our enjoyment of me we can really deal with the future. Nature sees the future as what I am experiencing now but also where I am headed. This means a key question regarding the future is whether it will be optimistic or pessimistic—or perhaps a combination. Looking to the future is why we need to think about how and where we will find hope, the focus of chapter 8.

## OTHER CULTURAL FORCES TO CONSIDER

This exercise helps us consider how each of the five key forces affect or shape nature. Nature has added a sixth for us—the future. These will help explain the stories and examples to be discussed. Before turning away from this hopefully not too esoteric discussion, we need to look at additional forces shaping the nature-culture relationship.

For culture the discussion is really a proxy for *relationships* in society and for the idea of community—how we approach our shared concerns for nature.

For justice the component is the idea of *rights and duties*—what are our rights to act or to expect and what are our duties in relation to others and to nature?

For democracy the keys are government and the processes public institutions use for citizens to act upon and relate to government.

For freedom the corollary is responsibility—how to insure freedom doesn't become a path to anarchy but instead is balanced by the ideal of collective responsibility

For the economy the main ingredients are value and wealth—how do we determine whether the economy is functioning well, are we staying ahead or losing ground?

For the future the key factor is our trajectory—which way are we headed, is it better for nature or worse and how well do we understand where we are headed?

## A LOESS HILLS EXAMPLE

To put these ideas into a grounded context, consider this example. Assume you own a 300-acre farm in the Loess Hills of western Iowa, comprised of grass and pasture, hills and timber, with some crop ground in the valley. The issue is its future. Its culture is agrarian and rural. Your freedom is the ability as owner to do with the land as you choose and make decisions for what comes next. Its nature is the steep hills, the unique landform and the scenic beauty enjoyed both from the ground and at a distance. Its economy is raising crops and cattle, using their productivity to measure the success of the operation. Its justice is a function of being privately owned, a status recognized as historic and privileged. Its democracy is how the community and local society choose to regard and respect both you as the owner and the land's natural features. Finally, its future is a function of how your actions as the owner are influenced by other cultural forces and whether the public and society choose to help shape how your land is used.

The point here? In *The River Knows* I wrote about the value of creating a LoHi recreational trail traversing the length of the Loess Hills and what it could add to Iowa's culture and our economy. But the truth is, it is not as simple as just saying Iowa's Loess Hills are unique and should be protected. Many people can agree on this. The process for protecting the Loess Hills is influenced by many other forces, all captured in the culture of nature. Unless the role and effect of all these cultural influences are considered, any effort to impose a scheme of protection and public use on the hills—and on the landowners will likely end with frustration, as did the efforts by the National Park Service to protect the Loess Hills several decades ago. When all the cultural forces are considered and all possible accommodations and compromises made, protection might be possible.

# Chapter 2
# Iowa's Nature: History and Threats

In summer 2024, a group of former students invited me to join them for a weekend at a cabin on Rabbit Lake north of the Twin Cities. The five close friends were all my students at Drake's Agricultural Law Center over 30 years ago. Since graduation they have gone on to careers as lawyers, politicians, business people, and lobbyists, but they have always stayed in touch and we have a special bond. For a number of years they suggested I join them on one of their annual summer getaways. Turning 70 made reconnecting with friends a priority, and an opportunity to visit the lake was inviting. Driving north from the Twin Cities, past the miles of shoreline on Mille Lacs, brought back memories of childhood trips when we would leave the farm in August and head north to fish at Big Lake near Bemidji. The weekend on Rabbit Lake was a wonderful opportunity to reminisce, catch up on their lives, and hear proudly told stories about families. These now included 12 children, many at college or beginning their own careers. It was an occasion to think about the passage of time and how we have filled our years. Of course, much of the weekend was spent boating on the water, sitting on the shore around a fire, enjoying our friendship.

The visit was an opportunity to consider how nature provides the fabric for friendship. Think about how nature activities provide places you share with friends and family. Many of your favorite outdoor ac-

tivities—fishing trips, hikes, bike rides, bird watching, and vacations—are most likely on or near the water. In all of these, nature is the calling card, the cause to get together, to "join us at the lake this weekend." Nature is the backdrop, the excuse for the shared time together. We often think of enjoying nature as a solitary activity, finding solitude on an evening walk or an early morning run. But it is important to recognize the powerful role of nature in cultivating friendships. Perhaps if there were even more opportunities to be active in nature we might be more connected to each other. Nature is the source of the social glue that builds friendships and community. Sharing nature with others can strengthen and sharpen our own appreciation for it. I have never taken my canoe on the river alone, in part for safety—it is always a shared activity, showing how nature helps build friendships.

Another insight from my visit to Rabbit Lake was thinking about the pull of water and its role in providing outdoor recreation and connections with nature. My drive north was filled with lakes surrounded by cabins, docks, and campgrounds. The highways were jammed with pickups pulling boats and jet skis, with trailers and RVs. The flow of people headed somewhere to engage with nature made me think about how many millions of us, American families, own lake homes or go to lakeside resorts and campgrounds for vacations, to get away. You may own a boat, trailer, or recreational vehicle. A large percentage of our population is invested in nature being there to visit, to enjoy, to recreate, to share with friends and families, and to pass on to the next generation. Given this truth, an important question for the future of nature is—Are we motivated enough or even well informed about what it takes to protect nature and to increase its availability? How well have we harnessed ourselves, we millions of outdoor enthusiasts, to speak for nature?

It seems obvious one reason Minnesota voters passed a law taxing themselves to create a natural resource protection fund was in recognition of nature's political and economic reality. Contrast our experience in Iowa, where 15 years after the IWILL amendment to the constitution to create the natural resources trust fund passed with 62% we have not seen any legislative action to increase the sales tax to fund the trust. In a political move that boggles the mind, in February 2025 a group of Republican senators, at the behest of Iowa Farm Bureau, introduced a joint resolution to repeal the Natural Resources Trust Fund amendment and replace it with a slush fund to lower property taxes. Thankfully the conservation community was able to quickly rally in opposition, and the idea was dropped, for now. The episode shows how the enemies of nature and public lands are ever ready to strike.

Surprisingly, strong public support for IWILL has not translated into any other effective public policies to protect the nature we still have, let alone acquire more. Could part of the reason for this lack of political support be because most Iowans have less connection and engagement with nature, less personal financial and psychic investment with it? Do we have less of the nature-culture connection discussed in chapter 1? Certainly there is evidence for investment in and advocacy for clean water in the Iowa Great Lakes. Their experience shows how important local recognition of the economic and physical connections to nature can be. The Okoboji Protective Association has thousands of members, but across the rest of the state this active public support for nature may be missing.

If we create more bike trails, hiking paths, and paddling streams will we see an increase in public support? Could it be a situation where the more you have the more you want? Perhaps one reason the Farm Bureau and others oppose efforts to acquire additional public lands and protect nature, is their fear if the public gets nicer parks and cleaner streams then citizens will want and expect more. As a result more private land might be "lost" to the public and the farming practices degrading nature—such as hog manure, odors, and water pollution—might attract increasing scrutiny and pressure for change. Viewed this way nature takes on a different form. Instead of being the beautiful place to recreate, restore, and connect with friends, nature becomes a battleground between public desires for more opportunities and private desires to make money, to act without oversight, and to not serve the public interest. As Frank Bruni notes in the *Age of Grievance*, this is in many ways a battle between different definitions of freedom. The role of grievance in today's politics is explored more fully in chapter 7.

## Nature's Voice

Greetings—nice to speak to you again. Since you have made it this far you probably know me quite well and are interested in my future. In that case, let me thank you for your love and support. As you may realize, my existence and presence in your lives doesn't require your active support or even awareness. No offense, but in reality I am here, always have been and will be in the future with or without you. It is always amusing to hear people say, "We need to act now to save nature." The truth is you need me to save yourselves. Having said that let me hasten to add I do very much appreciate your love, thoughts, attention, and actions. This is why it is an exciting opportunity to share my voice and perspectives on topics you will explore. I can use some friends and a bit more, no, make that a lot more, love.

Just like my mates the land and water, we have all taken some rough treatment in recent decades. Not by you necessarily, but certainly by your fellow citizens. You all know the stories—the impact of the bulldozers and chainsaws, the plows and draglines, the shotguns and dredges—all the many tools you employ to harness me to your service. Whether the clamshells in the rivers, towering pines of the north woods, prairies of the plains, or potholes of the fertile glacial lobe, all these and more have felt your touch, and not a gentle one I might add. To this list you can add the flocks of ducks, meadows of larks, fencerow badgers, and my favorite worker the beaver to the ranks of my congregants who have often been sacrificed on your altar of progress. But enough about my toils and troubles—you will encounter more of them as the professor shares his concerns. Today the story, my story to tell, is of hope. Hope is the world where I chose to live.

Yes, there are dark skies and threats of storms—your recent elections prove that in spades but there are also patches of blue sky and streaks of sunshine. I like to think you are part of the sunshine with your interest in me and what can be done to restore, protect, and enhance my future—our future really. So stay tuned for my voice, as I make appearances to comment on your actions: boneheaded ones like putting cattle feedlots near pristine trout streams or killing 60 miles of a river through a negligent fertilizer spill. I will also cheer on your brilliant ones—the good ideas like harnessing rivers for recreation, restoring my oxbows, and using prairie strips to plant among your crops. I will be here to critique your boondoggles too. Burying thousands of miles of pipeline through my fertile fields, to condense and ship a gas my plants can absorb, only to then pump it deep in the ground—all so you can skin me harder to raise more corn? Really! Who comes up with these crazy schemes? Clearly not people who understand or respect me.

## LEAVE IT TO THE BEAVER(S): NOT THE TV SHOW, THE CRITTER!

I am glad nature mentioned our friends the beavers. Here is one incredible part of the natural world. They may not be a keystone species, as the ecologists who study these things might say, like the wolf or the sea urchin, but they are a critical part of nature and for restoring it. For evidence you need look no farther than the wet meadows along the Yellowstone and in parks and ranchlands throughout the West, where owners and land managers have harnessed the energy and intellect of beavers to restore wetlands, create habitat, and repair the damage we have done.

Our appreciation for the wisdom of beavers wasn't always the case, as you learned in your early history lessons. Trapping beavers for their fur or trading with Native Americans for their pelts was one of the most powerful and lucrative enterprises in the early centuries of European settlement of North America. From the rivers of New England to the shores of the Great Lakes to the western mountain streams and all across the Canadian wilderness, beavers were trapped with little restraint. Thankfully the fashion for beaver felt hats waned before they were totally removed from the landscape, the extirpated fate we dealt to the passenger pigeon and almost to the bison. Given their flexibility and inventiveness, it's not clear that we could have eliminated beavers from the land, any more than we have done for the Norway rat, but thankfully we never got to test this hypothesis.

If you have even a modest interest in beavers and their incredible lives and history, I encourage you to read Leila Philip's, *Beaverland: How One Weird Rodent Made America*. It is an enchanting book, sharing not just the history of the fur trade of old and today, but also the author's passionate quest to establish a personal connection to the beavers living near her home. You will read fascinating stories, like the couple who welcomed a family of beavers into their home—one even sat to dine at the table, a family relation lasting for decades.

After reading *Beaverland* I purchased a copy for my friend Mike DeCook in memory of a conversation we shared at an Iowa Natural Heritage Foundation board meeting. The issue being discussed concerned a water drainage plan for a property we were acquiring. Mike said if it was his decision, he would rather hire a team of beavers than an engineering firm. He said the beavers would design and build smaller dams higher in the watershed rather than planning the one big structure we could expect the engineers to propose. In his opinion, the beavers' design would work better, they would build it at no charge, and they would maintain it—plus it wouldn't be over engineered and subject to cost overruns. The wisdom reflected in his view about the capacity and the role of beavers can be applied to many of our interactions with nature. It may sound simple, but the logic of "letting the beavers do it" is a lesson we can take to heart.

## What Price Have You Paid?

It may surprise you to learn that I read the newspapers when I can find the time—and watch the local news on television. No surprise but the weather portion is my favorite. It is always fun to see how well the weather people can predict or guess what I am serving up next. The September 8, 2024, *Sunday Des Moines Register* contained two excellent op-eds relating to Iowa's unfortunate situation with water quality and confined animal feeding operations. Chris Jones explained why your water quality is deteriorating and won't improve unless you change your ways. The piece by Tom Harkin and James Merchant examined the history of federal efforts to study environmental and health issues associated with confined animal feeding operations. Both shared a common theme—there are serious problems Iowans know exist but willingly ignore. The real question is: What are you willing to trade, some say sacrifice, in your future for near term gains? Boiled to its essence, the gain you seek appears to be simply the freedom to farm and raise livestock in any way you choose, free of worry that the public will say no. Do you ever ask: Is the gain worth it? The answers are becoming clearer every day. You are sacrificing the health of your land and water, the quality of life in rural Iowa, the future of small towns, and your children's futures. Some believe you are even trading your own health as well. This connection and the growing fears of cancer will be discussed in chapter 3.

Is what you have received in exchange worth it? Is the freedom to farm without fear of regulation worth the costs and risks? Is the freedom to inflict on your neighbors and communities the negative effects of however you want to treat the land worth the costs? If the rewards you reap are empty towns and closing schools, burgeoning cancer wards, declining farm numbers, shrinking farm incomes, and a farm sector eager to fight any consumer demand for better food and better care for livestock, then from my perspective you are losing the game.

Thinking this is your only future might leave you depressed—but there are alternatives. Niman Ranch farmers, for example, raise pigs in the manner they feel best, avoiding inhumane practices such as the gestation crates common in much of agriculture. Doing so helps produce some of the finest-tasting pork and earns premium prices, factors driving the demand for their meat. The same forward thinking can be found in the work of the Practical Farmers of Iowa, now with thousands of members. PFI holds a series of field days every summer across the state featuring families building more profitable, sustainable farms. You will learn more about Niman Ranch and PFI in chapter 4.

This type of farming might not be for everyone but they show that there are alternatives and reasons for hope - and reasons to support their efforts. Many of you fail to even admit there is a need for other, better ways to farm, or to acknowledge the health and environmental issues tied to many farming practices. You are unwilling to enforce laws to level the playing field so polluters don't have an advantage. Sadly your resources of land and water are being sacrificed because you are too timid and fearful. You don't have the courage to use the public's regulatory power to set common sense standards of care.

What if you invested in real answers focused on land and people, food quality, and communities rather than on billion-dollar boondoggles like the $CO_2$ pipeline to be funded with your tax dollars—all so you can prop up ethanol? Your only goal seems to be keeping your foot on the accelerator of farming practices, like using marginal land to plant corn with high doses of nitrogen and manure to degrade your land and water. Rather than university researchers striving to curry favor with their corporate paymasters funding the research, wouldn't it make more sense to use public funds and public universities to actually examine what is happening on your farms and to your health? Perhaps you could even try to understand why there are so many children afflicted with cancer to wave at on Saturday afternoon football games in Iowa City. As much as they may appreciate the wave, you know these families would rather be anywhere than on the receiving end of this feel-good gesture. You have the opportunity to seek a brighter and more hopeful future if you are willing to acknowledge what you are doing.

## ROAD TO HAMILTON: ALEXANDER HAMILTON, THOMAS JEFFERSON, AND AMERICA'S LAND

When I began the research and travel for this book *The Road to Hamilton* was still my working theme. Digesting Ron Chernow's masterful biography *Alexander Hamilton* helped fuel my desire to learn more about someone I had always considered a namesake and to visit the places where he lived and worked. One trip was to New York and Washington, D.C., in part to think about the role land played in shaping our early history and how Alexander Hamilton and Thomas Jefferson influenced our thinking. Clearly history has allocated to Jefferson the more significant credit for designing a system of landownership supporting wide distribution among relatively small landholders, fulfilling his dream that yeoman farmers would be the foundation of democracy. In contrast, Hamilton is often portrayed most directly as the friend of finance and manufacturing with less of a relation to ag-

26

riculture and federal land policy. There is truth in the distinction, but the differences between the two on the question of distributing the western lands are not as great as imagined.

In 1790, as the nation was dealing with how to allocate the western lands acquired by treaties with Indian nations, major questions before Congress were creating the public land office and the method of distribution. Several historic documents requested by Congress, from Hamilton in the Report on Vacant Lands from July 1790 and from Jefferson in the Report on Public Lands from November 1791, shed important light on these developments. While Jefferson argued primarily for agrarian development of the western lands to the exclusion of manufacturing, Hamilton argued for a more balanced view. He saw the need to develop manufacturing and industry as a way to support and create a marketplace for agriculture. Hamilton certainly understood the draw of land to people. The following quote is from his Report about Manufacturing from December 1791: "The desire of being an independent proprietor of land is founded on such strong principles in the human breast, that where the opportunity of becoming so is as great as it is in the United States, the proportion will be small of those whose situation would otherwise lead to it, who would be diverted from it towards manufacturing." And he said the same would be true for those immigrants drawn to the country by manufacturing who would find their opportunity in agriculture, a prediction borne out years later by the Homestead Act.

The important point here is Hamilton, like Jefferson, was in support of developing agriculture, but he knew it would be successful only if industry to support it and improve it was also encouraged. Doing so would open markets, both domestic and foreign, to absorb farm production. This historical comparison is important in understanding how the Northwest Ordinance and the land survey were developed and how land distribution played a critical role as the nation expanded westward. This was especially true with the handling of lands obtained in the Louisiana Purchase, shortly after Hamilton's untimely death.

The insight for us is how Hamilton and Jefferson and others of their era were dealing with nature as an open, blank canvas. Millions of acres and thousands of square miles, most of which they had never seen. They knew it was wild, natural, and open—full of riches in trees, grasses, furs, and soils—all waiting to be exploited. And did we ever. We harnessed nature and did with it as we pleased. Thankfully we didn't use it all and didn't destroy everything—but certainly large parts were tilled, bison were butchered, and former inhabitants were pushed further west. Slowly we learned our lessons or some of them—altering some of our ways, led by people like Theodore Roosevelt, Franklin Delano Roosevelt, John Lacey, George Bird Grinnell, Aldo Leopold, and Ding Darling. We came to see the need to preserve some of what was left and to learn to live with nature. We learned the importance of giving people the opportunity to have contact with and experience nature. From this grew many things—the national parks, national forests, the Izaak Walton League, the Boy Scouts, and the many groups who today focus on nature and the environment. Many of these developments are discussed in chapter 7.

Think of how our vision and opportunities, even our obligations, contrast with those of Hamilton and Jefferson. They were looking forward with little history to guide them. Our situation is in many ways the reverse—we are well down the road of exploiting nature and looking back; we know what we have done and how we have done it. We know the mistakes we've made, but thankfully, we are valuing the pieces we have left, the parts we didn't destroy. Now we are exploring what can be done to restore them, what parts can be reconnected, what new values and understanding can guide us, like turning to climate change.

We have no excuse for continuing to abuse nature, for destroying the remaining parts. We are not settlers, we are doing what we do now with full knowledge of our impacts. That is what makes actions like continuing to convert natural areas into croplands, bulldozing trees, and tearing out pastures and grasslands so frustrating and regrettable. We are still trapped in the box Leopold wrote about: we still view land and nature only in economic terms of how we might benefit financially with more corn or more ethanol or more new housing lots. Now to add insult to injury, agriculture argues that hundreds of miles of pipelines are necessary to pump $CO_2$ to North Dakota to save ethanol's future. If ethanol's fate is so fragile, how did we come to stake so much of our future on it? Isn't it time to realize we need to look for alternatives and identify the future? One sad reality of the $CO_2$ pipeline debate, the subject of chapter 5, is no one ever asks nature for its opinion, and no one appears to be looking out for nature. Does the Iowa Department of Natural Resources protect the rivers to be crossed? Is anyone looking out for the land? Eminent domain is all about the property rights of owners, but do we ever ask what nature and the land need?

This historical background, familiar if you attended Iowa's public schools, when we stilled cared about good quality education, help answer questions of "how we got the land, how we claimed the nation, and how we subdued nature." The questions create the modern opportunity to look forward through nature's lens. Doing so, we must recognize nature is looking back at our behavior—not just in how we enjoy and relate to nature but also in how we use and abuse it. The idea that nature is looking at us and measuring our conduct raises several more questions.

## What Nature Sees, From Us

While the good professor is waxing professorial, let me chime in and cut to the chase. What he is asking is, Why do some of you love me, and others not?

Some of you are very attached and connected to nature, yet many others are not. How and why did this happen? What explains these differences? Is it education, exposure, childhood opportunities, politics, religion, or self-absorption? Can any or all of these differences be changed?

When I look across your society, I see many contradictions, inconsistencies, and conflicts in your environmental concerns. You say you love me and want to save the planet from climate change and other global concerns. But it's not clear to me whether you are serious. When I look at the trends in your society, I am not encouraged. So many social developments seem to be diverting your attention, such as social media and its impact on children, the rise in home schooling, cryptocurrency and artificial intelligence with their demands for energy and water, sports betting, mixed martial arts, and the increase in online gaming. I'm also confused with all the tattoos these days. To me many of these are just distractions disruptive of human relations, separating you from connections with others and especially your connections with nature. They can create a hostile, even violent, social climate contributing to a lack of understanding of and connection with nature and the outdoors. Perhaps these are really nothing new, just a continuation of your consumptive, abusive, domineering mindset toward nature. The one you see reflected in your support of Big-Ag or Agra-nationalism, your attitudes toward the land, and your resistance to any form of environmental regulation. This helps explain events like the mess you created on the Nishnabotna River, an unfortunate but expected, tolerated, and possibly forgotten, even forgiven, tragedy. As the professor explains, is it just a cost of your "feeding the world" mythology? It finds a parallel in what appears to be your war on trees in rural Iowa. Enough with bulldozing out every fence line!

## The Nishnabotna River Fiasco

In March 2024, Iowans were shocked to learn of an unfolding tragedy on the East Nishnabotna River in southwest Iowa. As the days passed and more news emerged, the magnitude of destruction set in. The state suffered perhaps the single largest pollution event on a major river. Over 60 miles of river were devastated by a fertilizer spill from a storage tank operated by NEW Co-op in Red Oak, killing well over 750,000 fish and countless other creatures. The word "spill" doesn't quite capture the scale of what happened. Over the course of a weekend, over 265,000 gallons of concentrated 32% liquid nitrogen fertilizer, equal to 1,500 tons, or 3 million pounds, gushed out of a tank into a ditch and then into the nearby river. To help you picture the dimension of the spill, your garden hydrant flows at around 10 gallons a minute, so this "leak" was gushing at over 70 gallons a minute, all weekend! As the facts revealed, the cause was a valve that was not closed, apparently because the fertilizer had crystallized, plugging the valve, and any impoundment barriers were either nonexistent or ineffective.

You might say well, Professor, this was just a tragic accident and not the result of our cavalier attitude toward handling pollutants or protecting nature. Or you might say, at least the Nish is 150 miles away, so no skin off my nose. But couldn't the spill just as easily have happened on the Raccoon or the Des Moines? Could the Des Moines Water Works have protected its water supply from something like this? In *The River Knows* the Raccoon River told us what it knows, so I've asked it to say a few words about how it views what happened on the Nish.

Thank you, Professor, for the opportunity to comment about what has happened to my friend the Nish. As you can imagine, I am happy it didn't happen to me, but that is really beside the point. Here are three things I can say about this incident:

First, it was entirely predictable—and preventable if you cared more about protecting water quality.

Second, it could have happened anywhere in the state and on any river! What if it had happened in Perry on the Raccoon or in Ames on the Skunk or over on the Cedar? Rather than the poison flowing south to Missouri, it would have quickly overwhelmed your drinking water systems—then what?

Third, even more tragically but just as predictably, when it happened no one was in a position to come to the rescue or defend the river's honor. Sure the DNR responded and its local employees were outraged, but little to nothing has happened since. So much for your state's love of me.

It has been over a year now, and the sound you hear is Iowa officials sweeping the investigation of our largest fish kill and river murder under the rug. The spill killed most aquatic life for more than 60 miles downriver, as determined by DNR officials. More fish were killed in Missouri. The scale and devastation of the spill fed national and local headlines, but soon excuses began to emerge. As a native of southwest Iowa and the author of *The River Knows*, I found this senseless tragedy deeply offensive.

As provided in Iowa law, in April 2024 I wrote Director Kayla Lyon requesting the DNR investigate the spill and seek appropriate penalties and restitution. The law requires at least 25 signatures, but within a few days 62 others had signed from 18 counties. Our letter asked the DNR to request the nine-member Environmental Protection Commission to refer the matter to the Iowa attorney general, who under Iowa law can seek more significant fines and penalties than can the DNR. To our surprise, the EPC at its May 2024 meeting in Ottumwa voted unanimously to do so. And that is where things still sit today!

Since then no word—just crickets—from the DNR and the Attorney General. This is not unlike the silence of Iowa's Secretary of Agriculture Mike Naig and Governor Kim Reynolds, neither has made any public comment about the spill. This seems odd, especially given the magnitude of this blow to nature, with Naig being responsible for Iowa's much touted Nutrient Reduction Strategy and for regulating the storage of farm chemicals like the fertilizer involved here.

Three months after the May 2024 referral, when visiting the state fair I stopped at the Attorney General's booth in the Varied Industries Building and filled out a form asking for an update on the Nishnabotna investigation. That afternoon a voicemail thanked me for the inquiry, told me the Attorney General's policy is to not comment on ongoing investigations, and recommended that I call the DNR. Conversations with the DNR made it clear their fisheries experts were working to determine how the spill will affect future fish reproduction. As for enforcement or penalties, the referral means it is all now in the hands of the Attorney General's office. Over a year later no action has been taken.

My first job after law school 45 years ago was as Assistant Iowa Attorney General, so I realize legal matters take time. Who knows any day we might hear an announcement that NEW Co-op has agreed to pay a record fine for the fish killed and the other damages from their negligence. Or perhaps the U.S. Fish and Wildlife Service will enter the lists and take some action. Maybe the Iowa Department of Agriculture and Land Stewardship will even agree to enforce and tighten the rules for storing hazardous farm chemicals so this doesn't happen again on another river. Unfortunately the more likely outcome may be more delays, more time for sweeping it under the rug all in the hope this tragedy will slip from our memory. Only time will tell—but you can be sure nature has some thoughts to share on this event.

## Nature on No Justice for the Nish: Iowa Gives the River the Bird

Well, I do have to share some thoughts on this mess you created on the Nishnabotna River. I'm glad the professor gave the Raccoon the opportunity to speak about how this fiasco was so predictable and could have happened anywhere in the state. Isn't it about time you listened to the river or to nature?

I know one Iowan who hasn't gotten the message—the current occupant of your Attorney General's office, Ms. Bird. Even though she bears the name of a favorite portion of my flock, it doesn't appear the nature link has influenced her thinking. As I write, it is been over a year since the stewards of the NEW Co-op in Red Oak negligently killed over 60 miles of one of my rivers, as the professor has described. It has been over a year since your Environmental Protection Commission took the bold political step of voting unanimously to refer the case to the AG for action. So what legal enforcement action has your state's attorney general and Department of Justice taken, what punishment has been levied for this heinous crime, at least heinous from my perspective?

Nothing, not a dime, not a dollar—no enforcement action of any type—not even a request for an apology or a hollow promise not to let it happen again. How is that even possible?! Do you care so little for me, so little for the scale of my natural life killed, or the thousands of your fellow citizens affected?

Now it could be that your Ms. Bird is just too busy to get around to levying any justice for the Nish, what with her almost nonstop grandstanding agenda of filing lawsuits against any federal action or state law offending her MAGAnified standards for how society should function. The list of lawsuits is now in the dozens, and I don't want to give her warped political views credit by listing them, that is, with one exception. In late October 2024, Ms. Bird joined with Attorneys General from 24 states to intervene in a Ninth Circuit Court of Appeals case involving the Clean Water Act. The Ninth Circuit ruled in a lawsuit brought by the nonprofit Puget Sound Keeper Alliance against the Port of Tacoma that the Clean Water Act's provisions apply to the whole port operation, meaning it was potentially in violation and the lawsuit could proceed. Your Attorney General took great offense, saying the ruling threatens Iowa's farms and cities. In a press release concerning the request for the U.S. Supreme Court to hear the case, she said she fears the ruling will give "green activists the ability to impose burdensome mandates."

Her concern is the 50-year-old citizen suit provision in the Clean Water Act could be used to sue Iowa farmers and cities and force them to comply with laws protecting water quality. Maybe she fears some crafty Iowa lawyers might organize citizens and communities along the Nish to sue for justice. What an outrageous outcome that would be!

Her press release is both humorous and the height of hypocrisy. In particular, this portion—"State and federal governments are already enforcing laws to keep people healthy and waters clean. We must not allow unelected, green activists to weaponize lawsuits to force woke mandates, hurt farmers, or threaten cities that are working hard to keep drinking water clean." Wow—I didn't realize she cared for me so much! I must have missed the news about her actually doing anything to protect Iowa's water quality such as what happened on my Nish. Instead, to her this case from 1,400 miles away is just one more opportunity to gain another MAGA merit badge and wheel out her favorite hobbyhorse—the scourge of wokeness. Yes I know it sounds like a stretch, but according to your Solon of justice, citizens who desire to protect rivers and streams are an example of radical environmental wokeness. Silly me, I just thought they were people who care about their health and future, about enforcing the rule of law, and giving me a little love.

Perhaps we have discovered the true reason for Iowa's slow roll on bringing any justice to the Nish. Your Ms. Bird is afraid doing anything to actually enforce Iowa's water quality laws against a powerful agricultural business will cause her to be seen as being afflicted by wokeness. Being woke is in MAGA's eyes the new version of getting cooties—the ones you so studiously avoided on the playgrounds of your youth. So much for the search for justice—for the Nish or Iowa.

How do you think the Iowa courts will respond if someone brings a suit in the name of the Nish? What if the landowners and towns along the river have the courage to do so? Local DNR officials do care about the river, nature, and all the living things—the trauma was evident in their comments. But we are all adults and shouldn't fool ourselves into thinking state action will be either swift or adequate to address this crime. Do you think counting dead fish and tallying up a penalty is an adequate measure for the damages caused by killing 60 miles of a living river? Do we really expect the DNR, the

Environmental Protection Commission, or your attorney general in this politicized state to take serious action against a major agricultural cooperative or propose regulatory changes to prevent this from happening again? If so, then you didn't get the memo when the General Assembly passed a 2024 law, which the governor happily signed, to gut the authority of local governments to address storm water and soil related issues.

You may yet find out what the courts will do if asked to weigh in. In early March 2025 a group of local residents met in Red Oak to consider forming the Nishnabotna Water Defenders, in part to consider what legal options they might have. What might happen if Missouri sues Iowa for failing to prevent this? This reveals one of the final ironies about this sad story. Iowa has long been willing to export your excess fertilizers into the Missouri and the Mississippi rivers, so they can concentrate in the Gulf of Mexico and create a hypoxia zone devastating the livelihoods of shrimpers there. Perhaps all the spill on the Nish did was give you a taste of your own medicine!

# Chapter 3
# Buttons, Bunkhouses, and Cancer: How Iowa's Nature Ethics Threaten Public Health

If you have reached your 70s, you too have had the pleasure of looking back at your life and career. It is surprising to see how you filled the days and years and have now hopefully come to some sense of fulfillment. Looking back, I am struck by how important nature has been in providing the context and canvas for my life. Recollection is valuable, but it's only possible if we are alive—after that our legacy, if we have one, is what we have left for others. No doubt leaving a legacy is one reason, consciously or subconsciously, why people write books. You no doubt have experienced events, which upon reflection lead you to think, "Wow, I am happy to have survived that!" Perhaps it was a brush with cancer, a car accident, or another near miss with the hand of fate. One most clearly etched in my memory is the day I nearly drowned.

It happened on a late summer day in 1983 off the coast of Martha's Vineyard. As is obvious, I didn't drown, but not for lack of trying. If not for my friend Chris Halabi, I would have. We had anchored a friend's sailboat off a small island, and our party swam gracefully to shore, at least the rest of them. Nearing shore I floundered, my muscles seeming to seize up. My failing strokes were quickly overwhelmed by a growing panic. The thought "I am going to die right here" charged through my brain. Chris noticed my distress and nonchalantly swam back out the final 10 yards, took hold, and deposited me safely on shore. We may never have spoken of it in the days after, but in the decades since, his timely rescue has often come to mind. In the spring of 2024 on a research swing back East, I made the trip out to Connecticut where Chris lives with his wife, Carolyn. One purpose was to thank him and remind him of the episode. I wasn't really surprised he had no memory of the episode—clearly the magnitude of what hung in the balance wasn't seared in his memory as it was in mine. Regardless, I told him the story and thanked him for his effort, explaining how his gesture saved my life.

The second part of this story concerns learning how to do the sidestroke—a lesson in always having a fallback plan. Once we were on shore, the news of my limited swimming ability was shared with the group and how to get me back out the 40 yards to the boat was debated. Another friend, the source of our trip to the Vineyard, had the answer. Rather than trying to swim I should instead use the sidestroke, explaining if I did so there should be no problem making it back—and there wasn't! Ever since I have been a committed side stroker. Whether I'm in a friend's pool doing laps on vacation or at the YMCA staying in shape, the sidestroke is my choice. Here is a tip, two in fact—practice your sidetroke, it may keep you alive. Second, it pays to have a friend close by in any case.

## Nature's Thoughts on What It Needs

I hear much discussion about how you need to organize your actions so you can "save nature"—me! The underlying idea is I need you; otherwise I am in peril. I certainly do not object to having more friends concerned about my health. On the question of who needs who—who needs a sidestroke—it seems to me that you need me much more than I need you. All your new developments—artificial intelligence, server farms, social media platforms, and related developments, are interesting but more limited than you care to admit. None of these can grow a carrot or make it rain. For that you need me, and you need seeds, sunshine, water, soil, and a climate to support their growth. Plus it helps to have some human intervention of knowledge and labor. Knowledge is important because today it seems many people want breakfast but can't find the bacon seeds!

Don't get me wrong; there are certainly things I need from you. Here are some suggestions:

Care for me and respect me, acknowledge my contributions to your existence.

Understand how I work and the time required for natural processes to unfold.

Be considerate, careful, and frugal, not wasteful or profligate, when it comes to using my fertile soils, water, land, and other ingredients necessary for your food,

Speak up for me when I can't, when decisions may threaten my future.

It is so easy for you to take me for granted. Consider how much of your history is reflected in the idea I am limitless. There was more land, more trees, more bison, more mussels—all there for you. All you needed to do was seize them and to keep moving west if they ran short. You believed my resources were limitless, were renewable and self-reproducing. That was the idea until you came to the end—the edge of the continent, to the last of the bison, to the decimation of the mussel population. This didn't necessarily stop you—instead you doubled back and looked for alternatives and ways to work me even harder—this is where your technologies and genius come in. Many of you still believe I am limitless. For you I just serve as the backdrop for your lives rather than being the sea in which you swim and survive. Take away any of my elements—clean air, clean water, fertile soil, beneficial climate, healthy plants and animals—and then see how quickly your quality of life, your public health, even your ability to survive continue. I am patient, and if you are fortunate or wise enough to change your ways, I may be there to help you pick up the pieces—let me stress I may be.

## ALDO LEOPOLD AND THE ETHICAL SEQUENCE

In his famous essay "The Land Ethic," from *A Sand County Almanac*, Aldo Leopold begins with a description of the ethical sequence in developing relations in society. He notes the first ethic was the relations between individuals, as reflected in the Mosaic Decalogue or Ten Commandments. The second ethical evolution dealt with relationships between individuals and society. The Golden Rule interprets these relationships and our ideas of democracy integrate social organizations with the individual. Finally, he noted as yet there was no ethic dealing with our relationship to the land, the animals and plants existing on it, i.e., to nature (for most of us there still isn't). The rest of his timeless essay is Leopold's argument for why such a Land Ethic is elemental to human existence, "an evolutionary possibility and an ecological necessity." Much has been written about Leopold and the Land Ethic, an occupation I have been happily drawn to on many occasions. A recent road trip to a historic Iowa river town led me to think more clearly about all three of the ethics Leopold addressed.

The visit was to the National Pearl Button Museum in Muscatine, Iowa, known as the Pearl City during its reign last century as the world's capital for manufacturing pearl buttons. The opportunity came from the millions of mussels, referred to locally as clams, lining the bottoms of the Mississippi River and other midcontinent waters. What began in the 1890s as a small workshop-based family business punching out buttons from mussel shells had become by the early 1900s a major industry. At its height it employed over half the residents of Muscatine, producing over 1 1/2 billion buttons a year from 100,000 tons of shells harvested from the rivers. As you could predict, the rapid growth in button production soon overwhelmed the natural supply of mussels. Changing fashions, coupled with the development of plastics and other social forces led to the eventual decline, then the end of the once flourishing industry. This story is vividly captured in the displays and photographs at the museum, making it worth a visit.

When viewed in Leopoldian terms, the use and abuse of mussels were predictable. It was the classic American fable of employing, then exploiting, a natural resource available free for the taking, as was being done to the northern forests at the same time. On closer scrutiny, the button story and its relationship to Leopold's ethical sequence goes much deeper. One photo on the wall opens a window onto this relationship. It is in a display documenting the labor unrest in 1911 when legions of button workers organized a union and went on strike. The photo, pictured on the following page, is labeled "the juvenile sewers and carriers union of Muscatine, Iowa." It is a group shot of over 200 children employed in the button industry. Most of them were employed at home, sewing finished buttons onto the cards used by stores to sell buttons, cards provided by the factories buying finished buttons from the families doing the piecework.

Take a closer look at the enlarged portion of the front rows. You may be shocked at how young the workers are, many no more than five or six—girls and boys, brothers and sisters, at least one pair of

THE JUVINILE SEWELS AND CARRIERS, UNION OF MUSCATINE IOWA, 1911

twins, and one lonely African American child. They are not gathered on the school grounds or at a church picnic but as part of the workforce assembled to exploit the mussels. The exploitation grew far beyond mussels or nature, expanding to include the adults and families "employed in the trade" even to the point of exploiting their children.

Now think about the Leopoldian ethical sequence. Yes, it is clear there was no ethic extended to the mussels they were a gift from nature and the land. They were free for the taking and we knew no restraints. Exploiting them helped erode other ethics as well, ethics between individuals within families and ethics between individuals and society. It was individuals owning businesses who "hired" the employees, paying them as little as possible to get them to work the standard six days a week 10 hours a day. It was society approving not just these labor practices but encouraging, even expecting the exploitation of child labor, within the family context, all for economic reward.

When seen in this light the button story is a failing not just on the land ethic front but of all three ethics. This same reality is evident today in many of our conflicts involving natural resources and environmental conditions. A farmer's desire for yields can lead to abusing the soil through overuse of nitrogen with its impact on the public waters and the rights of other citizens to enjoy them. It is a $CO_2$ pipeline waiting to use others' lands, to have the action sanctioned and approved by society, and ultimately subsidized using economic resources collected from the public. At every turn you find an ethical challenge of the more powerful being able to exploit the resources of labor, water, money, and human dignity, all with nature—the land—providing the backdrop and context where we let it happen.

## LESSONS FROM THE "BOYS" IN THE ATALISSA BUNKHOUSE

Our willingness to overlook actions in our communities that damage nature or abuse animals is regrettable, but we shouldn't really be surprised. We often do the same or even worse when humans are the victims. Here we can find many examples, from domestic abuse and sexual violence to neglect of children and unsafe workplaces. Twenty years ago Iowans experienced a most shocking revelation and faced the ignominy of being complacent and complicit in the long-term abuse of dozens of mentally challenged adults. The sordid tale involved the infamous work of Henry's Turkey Service and the dozens of "boys" found living in squalor in the Atalissa schoolhouse. The victims weren't really boys; they were grown men, most with intellectual disabilities. Henry's had shipped them to Iowa years earlier, after "acquiring" them from state-run facilities in Texas, to do some of the most unpleasant jobs in a nearby turkey slaughterhouse.

Henry's held the state contract for their care and controlled their employment, but there were accomplices in the matter—the state of Texas, Iowa social service officials, the turkey plant employers, and in some ways the good citizens of Atalissa. Their story, both the sad details and the ultimate release, was vividly told in 2016 by Dan Barry in *The Boys in the Bunkhouse: Servitude and Salvation in the Heartland*. Not everyone in the story is equally deserving of the label villain, and thankfully the boys eventually found their heroes. Dedicated social workers knew something wasn't right and fought until higher-ups listened. Lawyers championed them in the search for justice and helped find them some form of compensation. Journalists played perhaps the most critical role, eventually being able to bring the matter to the public's attention, unveiling the truth, a truth known for decades by many who should have acted but failed.

Yes, the story is a sad one, but it does evolve toward a happier ending. The boys, many in their 60s, were eventually freed from what had been decades of modern slavery. Their advocates were able to use the tools of justice to obtain compensation so they could live out their lives with the independence we all seek. Some were able to reunite with the family members who had missed them for the many years they labored in the dark recesses of Iowa agriculture.

You might wonder, what is this sad tale doing in a hopeful book about nature? To me the connection and parallels are clear. Like the mussels pulled from the nearby Mississippi River at Muscatine until nearly decimated, the boys were just one more natural resource to be harnessed to make other people money, so greed could be served while their humanity was ignored. Like the sows in the gestation crates hidden from our view, the boys went to work before dawn shackled in their own ways to "working turkeys" at the slaughterhouse, out of sight, out of mind, just a lowly cog in the economic wheel. Not unlike the eroding farm fields or the silt-laden streams Iowans drive by every day. The town folks of Atalissa knew the boys were living in the school, just as their employers at the turkey plant did. Certainly some forms of small town kindness were extended to them over the years. But the mystery of what their lives were like in the rundown schoolhouse was masked from view by collective benign ignorance. Do we ask questions of those tilling the hillsides or polluting the streams? Of course not. It is not our job, it is none of our business, and we don't want folks nosing around us, either. So hills erode, mussels are harvested, intellectually challenged workers are used and abused. Nature, both wild and human, provides and life goes on. That is until the issue becomes so bad it can't be ignored or tolerated. Until someone realizes that what is happening isn't just wrong and unethical but also illegal. Once the public gains awareness and questions are asked, then the answers might be found. What is causing our cancer rates to climb, why are the rivers brown, why is the water never clean, why does the countryside stink? Only once we start to ask questions like these will we ever know the answers.

## Cancer in Iowa

Iowans were shocked by the news in 2023 that our incidence of cancer ranked us number 2 in the nation, just behind Kentucky, and our overall cancer incidence rate is rising the fastest. The headlines startled many and led to much head-scratching and many questions: how is this possible, and why are our rates of new cancers so much higher? Understandably much attention turned to agriculture but the issues run much deeper. What does Iowa ranking number 2 in the incidence of cancer mean for us? Here are several observations:

The number 2 ranking is frightening because it surprises us; it confronts and contradicts our complacency and confidence that Iowa is a healthy place to live.

The fact it involves cancer has a powerful effect, given the fears we have about what a cancer diagnosis may mean (even with the variety and improvement in treatments) and our anxiety—are we next? While there are no good cancers, clearly some forms are more survivable and less threatening than others that seem to be death sentences, like pancreatic cancer.

We are uncertain about how we should respond. If the cause is something like smoking, we can stop and society can regulate it to protect public health. But with many cancers the diversity of types and the broad uncertainty of causation leave us feeling both frightened and somewhat helpless. Do we change our diets, test our wells, change our wills, move away?

Feeling hopeless can feed what appears to be a lack of concern or even curiosity. If you don't know what you can or should do to change, then you may end up doing nothing. You just hope for the best and trust in fate. Perhaps this explains what appears to be the relative lack of urgency by many of Iowa's political leaders. Other than a tepid proposal from the governor to increase cancer research funding by $1 million—"because Iowans need answers not speculation"—there is little push for more research funding or special studies to examine the issue. We probably spend more on researching animal diseases and the maternal health of sows than on cancer—or on researching human maternity issues for that matter! Perhaps we fear what might be discovered and we don't want to deal with what the research may suggest we need to do.

Uncertainty about cancer's causes has several effects: First, it triggers a guessing game, is it pesticides on our food, nitrites in our water, radon in the air, binge drinking, genetics, or all of the above? Second, it gives those invested in activities that are potential candidates for attention the ability to say there's no proof we are the cause so please look somewhere else. In Iowa the issue most clearly involved is agriculture and the growing suspicion it may be partly to blame. Does our heavy use of agrochemicals or our abundance of livestock wastes and fertilizers lead to increasing nitrites in our water play a role? The lack of research linking direct connections gives agriculture ample cover to say "not us and how unfair of you to even suggest it!" Third, even so, some public health researchers believe agricultural practices are likely causes. Their premise is we may not know for certain but we know enough to change our ways. Predictably the lack of definitive proof places these experts in jeopardy of being labeled as alarmists or threats to the peace and prosperity of our farm economy. Their concerns include a fear that even suggesting such links may threaten what little research funding now exists.

The truth is we may never have the smoking gun, the direct link showing this practice is the cause of cancer. The multitude of factors involved, the timelines implicated, the apparent randomness of the illness as to whom and when it strikes, all make such specific linkages difficult and rare. If society is waiting to act until there is proof, we may never have it and as a result we may never act. For some this is the goal. If the lack of action means your industry doesn't need to change or you don't need to reconsider your activities, this is a good thing. Whether this is true for society is another matter.

The combined effect of these factors is to create an aura of uncertainty and unease. Of course life will go on. Fields will be tilled, crops planted, chemicals applied, and all the other actions that make up our daily existence in a farm state. We will go to the doctor, run our tests, and wait anxiously for the results. And most of us will feel the wave of relief when the doctor says everything looks fine. For those of us, myself included, who hear otherwise, the worries only deepen and a new journey begins, one with an uncertain end date. For Iowans the hope is perhaps the next national cancer report will show improvement. What a relief it would be if Iowa would drop in the polls from second to fifth or even 10th in the incidence of cancer! Won't that mean our worries can wane and our attention shift to more pressing matters? How about those Hawks?! (My friends, you can answer this question, you can guess what nature thinks.)

One positive development aided by the unfortunate cancer news involves considering how the food we eat may be an avenue to better health. Clearly food and nutrition are not new issues for society. What may be new is recognizing the link between healthy food and healthy soil. The premise is we need to have a better understanding of how we treat our soil—not just soil fertility and the microorganisms in it but also the nutrient density and quality of what we grow on it. Historically we assumed the quality of our food and its impact on our health were not directly connected to the land where it is raised. Even organic food may focus more on practices used to raise plants and animals than on soil health. New research is underway to determine if improving soil health can help improve our health.

## IOWA LEADS THE WAY IN NUMBER 2

There is always a danger in confusing correlation with causation. This is certainly true as we examine the Iowa cancer story, where one of the most important challenges is the lack of certainty about causes. News stories about Iowa's unexpectedly high cancer rates have led to much speculation about possible causes. It is perhaps only natural many eyes have turned to agriculture, given our heavy use of agro-chemicals. When we add in the water pollution of nitrites from excessive use of fertilizer and from manure spread on farm fields from our tens of millions of pigs, we can see the smoke, if not the fire. Given these two potential sources, it is understandable why many light bulbs are going on or at least blinking, among those who believe farming methods are linked to high cancer rates.

On the pesticide front, the main battleground is litigation and legislation involving the use of Roundup, commonly known by the active ingredient glyphosate. The product was brought to the market over 50 years ago by Monsanto, but was acquired more recently by Bayer through a multi-billion dollar acquisition. Undoubtedly the company has experienced some buyer's remorse since the purchase, given the billions of dollars in litigation costs, judgments, and settlements it has paid in lawsuits alleging use of Roundup caused the plaintiffs' cancers. The case results are a mixed bag, with the company losing some and winning more, though the costs are staggering. The value of the product to the company is apparent because it has not given up the fight to save glyphosate. In a masterstroke of public relations and marketing Bayer has been able to shift the argument away from whether the product causes cancer, it argues this link is unfounded by science or use of the product can be replaced by others. The new premise claims without access to glyphosate, American agriculture is doomed—and the world will face starvation. In other words, to save farming we have to save glyphosate. Farmers, their friends in business, and many politicians eagerly enlisted in this fight, pushing legislation to limit the company's potential liability. Don't get me wrong, I am not implying our politicians are bought and paid for, but it appears some can be rented by the hour.

The strategy is straight from the playbook used by the makers of DDT in the late 60s when Rachel Carson raised concerns in *Silent Spring* and improved science brought DDT into the crosshairs. We know how that fight turned out and can rejoice in the results—including the naming in 2024 of the once endangered but now resurgent bald eagle as the National Bird. American agriculture was able to survive and thrive without DDT as science moved on to develop less harmful pesticides. Now the fight is being waged, as you might expect, in the courts and in state legislatures. In Iowa a campaign is underway to amend state law to prohibit litigation based on state tort claims relating to a failure to warn. The goal is to limit litigation and require lawsuits about glyphosate's dangers—and labeling—to remain in the federal courts, where the outcomes may be more favorable and predictable.

The campaign is why drivers in the Des Moines metro see electronic billboards urging them to stand up for farmers to protect the future of agriculture by assuring access to Roundup. It is why readers of the *Des Moines Register*, unfortunately a dwindling crowd, see full-page ads to the same effect. The ads are paid for by the Modern Ag Alliance, a Bayer-funded front group claiming to represent 80 plus state agricultural trade organizations, united in what they see as a fight for the future of modern agriculture—Control Weeds Not Agriculture! It's not clear exactly how a 50-year-old weed killer merits being the poster child for modern agriculture, but such is the nature of our "modern" agriculture debate. As fate would have it, the current director of the Modern Ag Alliance is a former student.

If the attention shifts from the possible contributions of pesticide use to the connections between nitrites and cancer, the question of correlation or causation again comes into play. It is well known Iowa is the nation's leader in producing not just pigs but also laying hens. This means we have tens of millions of animals producing food products but also millions of pounds of wastes. Several years ago Chris Jones wrote a provocative article on what he described as Iowa's real population. Rather than just consider our 3.2 million people, he calculated the amount of animal waste, that is, poop, produced by livestock. Adding this to our human population yielded a population-manure equivalent of around 168 million people, a population density similar to Bangladesh. The news coverage of his writing included headlines like this gem— "Iowa ranks number 1 in number 2"—highlighting how the amounts of animal waste applied to our land contribute to water quality problems, especially high nitrite levels.

Current science is raising significant concerns about how Iowa's high levels of nitrites may be linked to certain cancers. As a result, the parallels with today's headlines concerning Iowa's cancer incidence ranking number 2 are clear. For most people cancer is their single greatest health worry. It is safe to assume you may feel this way. If so isn't it fair to say cancer is number 1 when it comes to health concerns? If true, then another way to look at these two issues is while Iowa ranks number 1 in number 2 for livestock poop, we also rank number 2 for number 1, when it comes to cancer as a human health concern.

## When Will You Learn? I Fear the Next Pandemic

In recent years you have been through a lot. I am thinking especially about the Covid pandemic years of 2020 through 2023 and all the disruption and uncertainty those brought. It was a traumatic and transformative period. For many of you the political winds of 2024 and the outcome of your presidential election were disheartening, leaving you anxious about what might unfold in the coming years. One spot of good news in all this is the comfort, relief, and joy I provided so many of you. The soothing evening hike, the weekend at the beach, the fishing trip to the lake, nature (me!) has been able to and will continue to provide the comfort to ease your minds and soothe your souls. I relate this story not just to toot my own horn, though I don't mind a little love. No, I remind you of this in part as a cautionary note, a timely reminder. One is necessary because you may be setting yourself up for another ride on the pandemic merry-go-round. This time it will most likely be a bird flu like H5N1 spreading through your poultry flocks, into dairy herds, your milk supply, and to the workers—and potentially to you.

Let me explain my concerns so you can understand how nature sees this. If you appreciate my concerns, you can consider what may need to be done. First, I must admit these pandemics are part of me, there is no use denying it. Germs, bacteria, viruses, and more are all part of me. There are many things out there and, yes, some are nasty and may even kill you, but they all are part of the cycle of life. I am, as you know—or should—self-correcting. Life evolves, resistance develops, and things go on. As proof, I still exist and you are alive to read this.

Good bacteria fight bad ones, antibodies overwhelm germs, fungi and mycelia break down organic matter to furnish nutrients to the soil to fuel new plant life. You get the point and you should know the score—you are an adult. Without these natural forces you would be surrounded by piles of your own wastes, succumbing to whatever germs you may have encountered.

Even with my ability to self-correct however we have to think about how these natural forces might become pandemics—just as you have to fear how my cell mutations can lead to the cancers plaguing you. Whether a new pandemic will emerge is in part a function of what you do and how you respond. When you wanted to stop the spread of mad cow disease you wised up and stopped feeding sheep brains and spinal material to livestock! The point is you need to consider the methods by which threats can spread and how they can be avoided, especially as it relates to food. How you raise livestock, how you house poultry and dairy animals, and how your meat-processing industry functions can contribute to the spread and distribution of potential illnesses in society. Your news regularly announces recalls for various foods—fruits, vegetables, leafy greens, and more—as a function of concerns for salmonella, listeria, or other potential contaminants.

How potential contagions spread· and how you respond by containing or treating them are all on you. This is largely out of my hands. The rapid pace with which you developed vaccines and eventually contained the spread of Covid was impressive and shows what you can do when you are motivated. Unfortunately, many people died from Covid—sorry about that—and the economic hardships and dislocations were perhaps greater than necessary. But you were able to get on top of it so life could adjust and return to a new normal. Your experience with the pandemic gave you a great opportunity to learn and be prepared for what may come next. Unfortunately, it is unclear what lessons you took away from this experience. The health benefits and value of vaccines are pretty clear, but the political backlash seen in the anti-VAX movement and the growing antigovernment reactions relating to business restraints, masking, and more are also clear and may have an even greater impact.

I saw these reactions reflected in the anger in the 2024 presidential campaign and the rise of the Trumpian antigovernment, antiauthoritarian, antiexpert response. Rather than hail your victory over Covid as a triumph for public health, it seems to have functioned instead to split you into those who believe in science and trust the government and those who believe in neither—and the neithers seem to have won! Enjoy your measles!

When you combine these developments with the preexisting antigovernment, "no rule for regulation" orthodoxy especially prevalent in agricultural and rural areas, you have a recipe for trouble. These attitudes are reflected in the resistance to developing effective water-quality programs and the resistance to the climate discussion. I actually overheard a group of farm leaders debate whether to call their actions climate-smart agriculture or just smart agriculture. You can guess what side won, you smarty!

Now the chickens are coming home to roost, literally and figuratively. As you read this, the United States is probably still dealing, arguably not well, with what has the potential to be your latest pandemic. It probably involves the movement of bird flu out of poultry flocks into dairy barns and through the infected cows into milk supplies and onward, potentially threatening humans. You have already experienced the economic effects with record-high egg prices and shortages. Now you are considering vaccinating the chickens! Funny how vaccines may be good for chickens but a threat to your kids!

Folks like to blame me when things like this happen. "It is those wild birds spreading the flu, there is the problem." Yes, wild birds can carry the disease, often with little impact on their own health, and they can be a vector for its spread. Just as likely a cause for any spread you experience is the movement of dairy cows and a lack of testing. Really any blame should go to your unwillingness to confront the political resistance to rapid government action and the reluctance of businesses that may be most affected to act. So you don't, until events on the ground become critical and you need to. Then the search is on for whom to blame and whom to sue, two of your favorite pastimes.

What you are seeing is the cumulative effect of your politics brought together:

You don't necessarily trust experts.

You don't want to give government the funding or regulatory tools needed to respond quickly, such as by testing dairy herds.

You don't want to invest in research and then connect the dots that might actually tell you what the cause is.

Farmers fear losing money if milk is considered contaminated or if herds or flocks are infected. So they resist government inspections and this resistance slows the response, meaning the diseases spread and the risks increase. The risks are more than farmers' economic losses they include the potential public health impacts.

The farmworkers involved are given little attention, in part because they are poor, unorganized, and often undocumented. If or when they become infected or the virus spreads through them this is not necessarily a priority for farmers, the industry, or arguably even society. Their health appears to be just another cost of doing business, a cog in the economy just like the boys in the bunkhouse.

The government agencies who have responsibility, like United States Department of Agriculture and Food and Drug Administration, are often hesitant to confront the farm and industry resistance. So they delay and hope for the best, offering happy talk and optimistic predictions about what they are doing and how well it may work. At the same time other experts, scientists and health professionals who deal with the spread of diseases, are busy issuing increasingly alarming concerns about what could happen. Are they crying wolf, are they just being naturally cautious, or are they warning you about something you should take much more seriously? You may soon find out, that is, unless by the time you read this, you already have.

The pattern you see is much the same—you are just repeating the ways you have dealt with environmental health and me— issues such as water quality, soil erosion, and land degradation, all the traditional worries about how you treat the environment. Now your bad habits are being repeated with the potential for how you address the possible health risks from a new pandemic. Rinse and repeat the question I asked you at the start: "When will you learn?"

# Drinking Alcohol Is Honoring Nature

Do you ever stop to think how prevalent drinking alcoholic beverages is in society? Consider how many bars and taverns there are in your town or restaurants and cafés selling beer and wine. It's pretty amazing when you think about it. Not to mention the countless grocery stores, gas stations, liquor stores, big-box discounters, and everywhere else you can buy alcohol to enjoy at home, with friends, at the lake, wherever—though usually not at work! It is probable you are like me and enjoy a nice drink now and then—be it beer, wine, cider, or the harder stuff as they say. There are as many options as there are opportunities. My favorites are a nice bourbon or glass of zinfandel, or even a fine cider, unless it is summer, then give me a gin and tonic. The surgeon general has certainly thought about the prevalence of drinking, and in the latest turn in the revolving science about the health impacts of drinking has proposed new labels to warn us that any amount of alcohol contributes to an increased risk of cancer. Good luck with that!

Think about where you often enjoy a nice drink. Assuming you aren't sitting in an airport or a hotel bar or out to eat with friends, there is a good chance your favorite place to imbibe is outdoors, surrounded by nature. Sipping a beer on the dock waiting for a fish to bite, enjoying a cool one down on the beach, or a glass of wine on the patio or deck. The truth is, drinking alcohol often goes hand in hand with nature, a connection worth our consideration.

It only makes sense that drinking goes so well with nature, because nature is really behind every drop we drink. The grape juice vinted into wine, the pure water blended with malt and grain to brew beer, the apple juice fermented for cider, and of course all of the agricultural ingredients used to distill liquors. From the corn in the bourbon to the potatoes in the vodka, from the botanicals in the gin to the agave in the tequila, every version and every drop of the alcohol we drink are both products of nature and an opportunity to celebrate it. I think this is one reason places serving alcohol are so popular and present in society. Now if you are a teetotaler for any reason, always have been or now need to be, this of course doesn't mean you can't love and enjoy nature. The point isn't that alcohol is a required ingredient to honoring nature. The point is that nature is a source of alcohol and our pleasure in enjoying its flavors and effects is natural and should be honored as such rather than resisted, suppressed, or shamed.

The ubiquity of alcohol and its everyday role in our lives are just more evidence of how nature shapes us. The connection between drinking and its relation to nature came to me one day, where else, but sitting in a bar studying the ranks and rows of bottles arrayed in front of me, like this bar in Ashville in the photo below. I was struck by the

almost religious symbolism of the display. That's when it dawned on me—drinking, or as I like to see it now—enjoying nature's gifts—is really its own form of religion for many. Sitting at a bar enjoying a beverage has a parallel to sitting in church listening to a sermon. For both you let it sink in and fill you with its effect. Think about it for a moment—are the adults you know more likely to have visited a bar in recent months than have attended church? If you said bar, the data support the idea more people are likely to have visited a bar to enjoy nature rather than been to a place of worship. Even those who may not frequent bars may enjoy a drink or share a bottle of wine while dining with friends. You don't need to be in public to enjoy a drink. Consider all the beer, wine, liquor, and more enjoyed in the comfort and privacy of wherever you call home for the night. Is this really any different from saying prayers before a meal?

Now you might think the good professor is making this up on the fly, perhaps to cover his own drinking! Here are some numbers to consider. Recent reports indicate 62% of American adults report drinking alcohol, while 38% abstain. This number has changed little since the late 1930s fluctuating between the high 50s and 70%. Drinking increases with income—80% of people in households with incomes over $100,000 drink while only 49% of households with incomes of less than $40,000 do. The 2020 census reports we have 331 million people and 78% of them are adults, meaning there are about 258 million adults. This means at least 160 million adults regularly enjoy drinking alcohol. In 2023 it was estimated there are 63,000 taverns and bars in the U.S. and the bar and nightclub sector accounted for over $37.6 billion in activity. Total sales of alcoholic beverages were estimated to exceed $260 billion or about 3.4 billion cases, with beer accounting for 44%, spirits 40%, and wine 16%.

When it comes to religion there are estimated to be around 380,000 churches, according to a 2020 National Congregations Study survey. The number of adults who report attending church weekly is around 21% with another 9% reporting attending almost as often. If these numbers are accurate, over 55 million Americans may attend church regularly. The "may" is important because other research suggests the self-reported numbers may be greatly inflated, with real church attendance rates closer to 5 or 6% of adults—or 20 million adults. In 2023 total charitable giving in the United States was $557 billion. Of this, religious giving accounted for $146 billion. When you make some comparisons, it appears at least three times as many adults drink regularly as attend church regularly, if not more. In addition, sales of alcoholic beverages exceed religious giving by well over $100 billion a year.

So what can we make of these numbers and these comparisons? As little or as much as you might like to. My point in making them isn't to disparage religion or deny the important role it plays in many people's lives and in the shape and economy of our nation. When you visit a bookstore you have probably noted the many aisles of books on religion, even the oddly named "religious fiction" section. Organized religion's history of abuse, fomenting conflict, restraining individual freedoms, and causing and justifying wars is another matter, but those are bones best left to be picked over by writers more interested in dissecting them.

Because my focus is on nature, the key point about alcohol is we need to recognize it and honor it as part of our traditions and our relationship with nature. Rather than moralize about the evils of demon rum, let's drop the charade and admit humans can and do enjoy drinking. Rather than trumpet the possible health dangers of even moderate alcohol consumption in our effort to promote wellness at any cost, let's admit that ultra-processed foods and the ubiquity of pesticides in our diets may pose equal or greater risks. Trying to deny adults the opportunity to enjoy a drink while serving them a plate full of guilt is an example of the nanny state. It ignores human nature—and nature. It is the personification of H. L. Mencken's comment "the haunting fear that someone, somewhere, may be happy." Don't get me wrong, clearly alcohol abuse can have deadly effects—drunk driving fatalities, cirrhosis of the liver, and ruined lives and broken homes. Research on alcohol and cancer links deserve attention. But driving cars, climbing ladders, and countless other daily and normal activities all carry risks of injury and death. Any of the risks from drinking alcohol should be weighed against its important role in connecting humans to nature in enjoyable and profitable ways. The key is to respect nature when you hear its call. Right now I hear it saying it's time to honor nature and enjoy a nice drink.

# Chapter 4
# Agriculture: Nature's Biggest User or Abuser?

When we think about our relationship with nature and agriculture it is important to recognize we cannot escape two fundamental requirements. First, producing food someone wants to eat. Second, we must recognize this is possible only if we have the land, soil, water, seeds, animals, knowledge, climate, and labor we need. Much of modern agriculture is spent searching for new technologies and new methods to try to increase productivity, essentially ways to "improve on nature." Certainly this can be an important goal, but we can't ignore the two fundamentals: producing food and having the land on which to do it sustainably.

Last winter found me immersed in a series of books written about thievery. There was *The Orchid Thief, The Map Thief, The Book Thief, The Art Thief, The Falcon Thief, The Feather Thief, The Porcelain Thief,* and even the *Tree Thieves*—who knew there were so many thieves! All the books were fascinating in their insights into human nature and our darker sides. If you want to pick one to sample the genre, my suggestion is *The Feather Thief: Beauty, Obsession, and the Natural History Heist of the Century* by Kirke Wallace Johnson. Reading the books made me ponder, Who are nature's thieves? In some ways I am trying to address this question in this book. Given our focus on Iowa, my immediate attention turns to farmers and agriculture.

Much of my career has been spent as a nature crimefighter, trying to push back against those who either abuse nature or ignore it. *The Land Remains* and *The River Knows* flow down this stream, as do my 30 plus years on the Iowa Natural Heritage Foundation board, my over 20 years on the Leopold Center's advisory board when it existed, and many other activities, such as recent service as a soil and water district commissioner for Dallas County. One important ingredient missing in Iowa is how we don't actually use this label or treat people as thieves or even consider their actions to be thefts. Our "Iowa nice" attitude, the "we love farmers and capitalism" approach to the world as reflected in the ubiquitous ANF (American Needs Farmers) logos, seemingly render us incapable of calling out bad behavior, even when it is apparent. Farm groups love to talk about penalizing the bad apples who cause problems and give farming a bad name, but we just never find any in the barrel.

Perhaps many of the actions against nature described in this book are not thefts in the legal sense of the word. The unfortunate reality is often the conduct is legal, even officially sanctioned. This means the General Assembly and the state's politicians are members of the crime ring, too. Effectively though, many of the actions are thefts. They steal directly from nature and from the services it provides society. Bad farming practices steal from the public by taking natural resources to use for private consumption. They steal our soil, our water quality, and our ability to enjoy nature, and they steal from the future, from those who follow.

One reason we are unwilling to call these actions thefts is because we don't want to offend, accuse, or blame the offenders. Doing so would require us to consider what next steps to take to punish them, another step society is unwilling or unable to take. Instead, we just accept their acts as how things are and expect or hope others, possibly agencies like the DNR or the soil and water conservation districts will do the job. What might be gained by changing the terms of reference and beginning to identify the actions as thefts and the actors as thieves? Would it be too incendiary? Can we assume anyone's response will be to say, "I'm sorry, how can I atone for my sins?" Probably not. Instead they will push back, harden their views, and go on the offense against nature—and its advocates. For evidence, in late 2024 promoters of the Summit Carbon Solutions pipeline, to be discussed in chapter 5, sent warning letters to six pipeline opponents threatening legal action if they didn't retract and apologize for statements the company believes are defamatory. Such fragile flowers these billionaires! I wonder if my lawsuit might be next once they read this book?

If we can't expect to change the minds of the bad apples, that is, the thieves, perhaps the audience for change is the public. Why do we allow this to go on? Why do we tolerate it? How do we expect a healthier nature if these antinature actions are legal, sanctioned, and sometimes even encouraged by public funding? If the thieves themselves are blameless then doesn't it mean we should be willing to accept some of the blame for corrupting them?

## Nature on Why We Fail to Act

I notice how you love me, at least when I serve your purposes. When things go wrong, like the mess you created on the Nish, it is a different story. Then it seems the only official response is the sound of crickets. Contrast this to what happens when my weather acts up and strikes out violently. It is only natural that storms and tornadoes happen in the spring. But when this happens, everyone rushes to help the victims, it's always about you all the time. I'm sorry much of Greenfield was destroyed by one of my storms and am saddened several good Iowans perished, but that is nature. I wish I had the answers and could tell you everything causing pain and discomfort to humans is under my control and I can remove them, but that's not the case. I believe your God would give the same reply. Neither of us has all of the answers. I can't claim to prevent cancer or to cure diseases and the causes of many ailments like ALS and MS elude both you and me.

However, there are many relatively easy and affordable steps you can take to increase your physical and mental health, and many of them are thanks to me—you are welcome. You could certainly exercise more and eat more healthful diets. Those are just two relatively easy steps you could take. Many other actions can improve your health and mine. Some of my best friends are people who write about me, people like Richard Louv, whose *Last Child in the Woods* brought much needed attention to the value of giving children the opportunity to know me. His *The Nature Principal* helps you think about the many benefits available from connecting to the natural world. There is Douglas Tallamy, whose *Nature's Best Hope* is full of practical advice for how you, especially you homeowners, can change your landscaping habits to unlock millions of acres of natural habitat. According to Tallamy, Americans could create as much natural land as is in your national parks—30 million acres—if you would just quit mowing half your yard. You know—the lawn of grass you insist on fertilizing, then mowing, and then fertilizing again, all so you can do more mowing! Who has brainwashed you into thinking this is a good idea? Does the Scotts Company Miracle-Gro hold a lead line on your soul? Do you own stock in John Deere?

# IOWA'S NEW THREE SISTERS

In the history of Native American culture, the three sisters are powerful reflections of traditional foodways indicative of agrarian insight and natural harmony. The three sisters were corn or maize (what Europeans would label Indian corn), pole beans, and squash or pumpkins. The three crops were typically planted in a raised mound, the cornstalks supporting the beans and the squash leaves shading the soil. Planted together the crops provided mutual support, shade, and even fertility, producing a nutritious bounty to enjoy in many ways over extended periods. Some ears of corn could be eaten young and fresh early in the summer; others were allowed to mature with the grain stored for the coming winter. The same was true for beans, delicious fresh or dried for later use. Squash or pumpkins could be eaten fresh or sliced and dried for stews. The squash blossoms could be enjoyed and the plentiful seeds dried for eating. The versatility and mutual benefit of the crops help explain why the three sisters legacy retains its power as a descriptor of native agriculture and an accessible way for today's gardeners, teachers, cultural historians, and others to honor the tradition. Three sisters plantings were endemic among the tribes living in Iowa and the Midwest, making the tradition perhaps the most identifiable link between the farming and foodways of our earliest inhabitants and today's consumers. The mutual dependence and sustainable circularity of the three sisters show the genius involved. All the sisters—corn, beans, and squash—remain important and popular parts of our foodways.

The legacy of the three sisters came to mind as I was thinking about modern farming practices widely used in Iowa. Then came the epiphany; today Iowa has adopted a new three sisters style of farming, though one with a darker and more concerning impact on our future. What are the new three sisters? Ethanol—produced from our burgeoning corn crop. Glyphosate—and the other pesticides used to grow the corn. Hog manure—produced by the 20 plus million pigs fed on the corn and spread on millions of acres of farmland to help fertilize the corn. We grow more corn to produce more ethanol, we use more pesticides to grow more corn, and we raise more pigs to produce more poop, to help raise more corn—and the cycle continues.

Just like the traditional three sisters, each of these crops depends on the others to prop them up to promote their growth. However, the crops they yield are not nutritious life-supporting foods. Instead Iowa's new three sisters are technologies and products carrying their own baggage and environmental risks. Our addiction to ethanol leads us to consider outlandish boondoggles like burying miles of pipeline to carry $CO_2$ sequestered from ethanol plants and to resist the movement to electric vehicles. Our dependence on producing corn, and its monocultural first mate of soybeans locks us into heavy reliance on agrochemicals like glyphosate. The crop production causes erosive soil losses at levels that have hardly budged in the last three decades. Our warm embrace of hog production with the attendant millions of pounds of manure, coupled with our unwillingness to address water-quality impacts of manure handling, contribute to degrading our water and polluting the air, corroding the quality of life for many in rural Iowa. Yes, there are economic benefits associated with all of these new sisters. If there weren't, we would be even greater fools than one might guess. But questions remain. What exactly are the benefits and who enjoys them? What are the associated costs and risks, and who bears these? What are the alternatives Iowa might embrace if we were not shackled to these three sisters?

# Agriculture and Farming: Public Servant or Public Enemy?

Reading Dan Egan's *The Devil's Element: Phosphorus and a World Out of Balance* about the role of phosphorus as a water-quality concern raises several questions—not just about the impact of agriculture but about the role farm states like Iowa play in these national issues. His concerns deal largely with water quality such as the role of hypoxia in the Gulf of Mexico (its name now and forever), the contribution of nutrients coming down the Mississippi River from Midwestern farm states, and the Clean Water Act exemptions for agriculture. The imbalance of how we treat point sources, such as municipal sewage systems, and nonpoint sources, such as what runs off farm fields, is nonscientific and indefensible from an economic and even a political perspective.

The real issue that struck me after reading Egan's book is the wide gap between the self-image and perception Iowa farmers have of their work (and worth), an image shared by many Iowans, and what may be the reality of their impact on the public. This gap may increase as public skepticism grows and our willingness to accept agriculture's explanations wanes—with the potential for major political and economic effects on the future of agriculture. When you think about the self-image most farmers have, it is one where they see themselves as public servants, raising food, caring for the land, sacrificing to make it healthy and sustainable, all in a sense of benevolence. There is truth in this vision, but unfortunately the full story is much different. Farms are not charities and food is not raised from a sense of benevolence—it is all about economics and money.

Consider Iowa agriculture and how we revel in the glow of being the leader, the number 1 producer of corn, hogs, egg layers, and ethanol.

But each of these stories has a darker side at a national level, raising less flattering impressions. Our pursuit of ethanol resulted in the Renewable Fuel Standard mandating most gasoline sold in the U.S. contain 10% ethanol or E-10. Now corn lovers and farm state politicians are pushing for E-15 at a national level, an even more dubious energy strategy. Ethanol raises real environmental questions about how and where we grow corn and highlights ethical dimensions of the food or fuel issue and the increasingly costly federal subsidies to underwrite farming—the so called safety net of publicly funded welfare payments to farmers. When you add in ideas such as the $CO_2$ pipeline, discussed in the next chapter, to support a future market for ethanol, the picture becomes even cloudier.

Our continuous expansion of corn and soybeans, not for food but for fuel, raises many questions. The direct impacts are rising land prices and fewer opportunities for new people to farm, as well as the overuse of nutrients, the impact of soil erosion, and soil health degradation. Similarly, our push to increase producing egg layers raises animal welfare concerns and health issues for workers. The economic risks are from avian influenza outbreaks and the reluctance to adopt alternative production systems. Iowa's longtime love affair with hog production is associated with significant water-quality and pollution problems from handling manure and the impact of odors and leaks on neighbors.

Finally, there is the issue of costs to the public through price supports, direct farm payments, crop insurance subsidies, and disaster relief when prices decline or the weather harms agriculture. These add up to billions of dollars each year, going to a relatively small group of individuals—in Iowa it includes roughly 20,000 large farm operations, most with millions in net worth. For example, in late March 2025 the

USDA announced Iowa farmers would soon receive $900 million in welfare checks to help make up for lost incomes over the previous two years. Did you get a check? This is nice work if you can get it.

The public is essentially subsidizing a system that causes significant environmental and social damages, with the financial benefits going to a relatively small group of people. The justification offered is this laundering of money through farmers is essential to support the social and business environment for agriculture so that everyone else—from bankers to landowners, seed corn companies to fertilizer dealers—get a lick on the cone of public money we serve farmers. I recently asked an audience of Iowa farm managers and realtors why we are willing to turn farmers into the nation's largest group of welfare recipients? The response was mostly silence and uncomfortable seat shifting.

At the same time, the farm sector operates largely free from any regulations to limit its environmental impacts, such as the Clean Water Act exemption for agricultural pollution, and the now essentially nonexistent soil conservation enforcement provisions from the USDA. The agricultural community greets today's public concerns and expectations about climate with three prerequisites: any programs must be voluntary, not involve regulations, and offer compensation. That was when climate change was still a topic for adult conversations, before the new administration came to power and banished any mention of the C word from official actions.

The point of this listing is to illustrate the sources of the gap between agriculture's self-image and what may be the reality of changing public perceptions. One puzzler is why agriculture is so willing to pick what appear to be bad fights? First Iowa sued California to prevent it from enacting rules requiring laying hens to have more room—and lost, several times. Then the state sued to prevent California from implementing rules outlawing gestation crates for sows—and lost all the way to the U.S. Supreme Court. Now Iowa is lining up to fight the movement to electric vehicles and prolong the life of ethanol with E-15 and $CO_2$ pipelines. We have enacted laws to prohibit the sale of cell-cultured meat if the M word is used to describe it. All these essentially futile efforts to support the status quo make me wonder if the state will ever pick a good fight—like cleaning up the water, protecting the soil, or improving public education?

## WHERE ARE THE BENEFITS OF ETHANOL?

Ethanol and biofuels are in the news with the future of the farm bill, the $CO_2$ pipeline controversy, and now sustainable aviation fuel. If you think about it, over the last two decades when has ethanol not been in the news? Regardless of the issue, the answer to any attempt to question the future or value of ethanol is the same. Ethanol "is so important to Iowa we can't possibly live without it." Think about this for a moment. Can you explain why ethanol is so important to Iowa or to you, so much so we cannot forgo any benefits we receive from it?

For something considered to be so universally important, you would expect the benefits to be equally clear. Certainly one comes to mind: the impact on the market for corn and the effect that higher corn prices have on land values. Here we have some evidence of benefits, though a bit of a mixed bag. In recent years, corn prices had climbed to the point where corn growers were actually making real money. These profits helped fuel investments in new equipment and technologies—and increase competition to buy or rent more land, driving up prices. One of the most immediate effects was to rapidly inflate the price of farmland. Increasing the price of farmland has the effect of increasing the rents landowners expect from tenants. This means much of the gains from higher corn prices are absorbed by landowners, not by farmers, especially because rented ground makes up over half of Iowa's farmland. Corn prices certainly increased at times in recent years, but today the story is much different with corn selling below the cost of production. Low commodity prices lead to rapid declines in farm income and not surprisingly to political demands for even larger public subsidies to make up the losses—like the $900 million just described. This all happened before the new president launched a trade war with our largest foreign grain purchasers, promising even more turmoil and more demand for payments.

One constant during all these economic fluctuations is the amount of Iowa's corn used in producing ethanol, around 60%!! So what is the answer? Does more ethanol lead to profitability for corn production or for losses from surplus corn production? Is the answer in either case to just continue producing even more ethanol, as Iowa's political and farm leaders seem to think? The reality appears to be ethanol may not have as much direct impact on farm profitability as imagined, with the real drivers for farm incomes coming from the larger functions of the economy: world demand, monetary policy, tariffs, and changes in the energy market. In terms of farmland prices, they have continued to increase, but the rate of increase has slowed and perhaps even peaked. If you are a landowner, ethanol has no doubt been positive. The real risk is what will happen to land values if the rug of public support is ever pulled out from under ethanol, like removing the Renewable Fuel Standard requiring gasoline refiners to include 10% ethanol in their products, a long-standing goal of the petroleum sector. Propping up land prices is the foundation card in this stack.

If ethanol is such a boon for our state, as the governor, our secretary of agriculture, and many others claim, you would expect the benefits to be visible in a healthier state. There are several hundred jobs in rural Iowa at ethanol plants and we have created a market for the surplus corn we grow. This has propped up land prices and increased farm income, most of it laundered through banks, landowners, input suppliers, and other businesses, the real beneficiaries of our farming system. What about the other possible benefits Iowa might have expected from ethanol? The evidence here is decidedly mixed. Few can argue rural Iowa or even our state is healthier or stronger than when our addiction to ethanol began thirty years ago. If you doubt my conclusion, ask yourself these questions about what has Iowa gained in recent decades:

Are our universities stronger or the costs to students lower, and has their research capacity improved, especially when funded by the public?

Are our public schools better funded, or have we eroded support for public education by siphoning off hundreds of millions of tax dollars to support private schools?

Have we funded a robust and effective water-quality initiative and increased stream monitoring so that we know where problems exist?

Did we fund IWILL, the natural resources trust fund approved by 62% of voters in 2010, to improve the public's access to nature?

Do we fund the soil conservation districts to give local county institutions the staff and funds to help landowners and farmers protect the soil?

Did we improve Iowa's social safety net, eradicate hunger in the state, and address problems of child poverty?

Did we improve rural health care, so county seat hospitals can stay open and expectant mothers don't need to drive 100 miles to give birth?

Did we make broadband access widely available so rural and small town residents have access to the electronic highway shaping our future?

Are these unreasonable goals for citizens to expect? Look at the questions and provide your own answers. The truth is we have not made much progress, if any, toward these important goals. In many ways our state has become more impoverished. We may have a new state motto, "Freedom to Flourish," but the emphasis is more on freedom and less on flourishing. We drove up corn production, tilled up more fragile land, and applied more fertilizers and pesticides, some of which find their way to our waters. All these actions were taken in the context of growing more corn to produce more ethanol, but the benefits are phantoms. Look around and you will be challenged to see many gains for our communities or the land. When we return to the question of what Iowa gains from ethanol, for something assumed to be so important, the answers are much less clear and sadly much more political.

In the spring of 2023 on an Iowa Farmers Union lunch and learn Zoom call, Chris Jones said that ethanol has to die if there is any hope to having cleaner water in Iowa. I had never heard him say this so directly and it certainly pleased the listeners. My first reaction on hearing him say this was to question his judgment because it is such a provocative statement. But the more I thought about it, I was struck by how few people are willing to challenge the constant barrage of claims made by politicians like Governor Reynolds and Ag Secretary Naig— and Democrats as well—about the benefits of ethanol and the largely illusory benefits you have just read about. Ethanol's legions of supporters might find comments like Chris' heretical but perhaps what the state needs is a little more heresy when it comes to accepting as true the claims made by the "all corn all the time" brigade.

Even so you have to recognize there are dangers in being a heretic. I know and admire Chris Jones and consider his commentaries on our situation in Iowa as very insightful. Arguing ethanol must die is a provocative statement sure to inflame its supporters.

The problem is ethanol is not going to die—at least not soon or of natural causes. I'm not even sure we could kill it if we wanted to. Politically and economically the deck is stacked for it to continue. Consider the policies we have in place to support it: the Renewable Fuel Standard; the move to E-15 availability year-round, an idea politicians of all stripes and parties seem committed to; federal commodity programs and crop insurance subsidies to support corn production, and maintain land prices; projects like the proposed $CO_2$ pipeline and other policies to encourage carbon contracting by farmers; Iowa's 40 plus ethanol plants producing several billion gallons of ethanol each year and employing hundreds of people, and the market for over 2 billion bushels of corn (60% of Iowa's crop) annually; along with U.S. energy goals, to promote "biofuels" like "sustainable" aviation fuel.

This list explains why ethanol won't die. In the near term, it would be an economic disaster for Iowa and Iowans if it did. Land values would fall, commodity prices would tank, and the farm economy would falter even more if the market for ethanol were to disappear quickly. A different question is: Can we wean ourselves from it over time? Efforts to diversify agriculture, with more focus on environmental protection and water quality, more support for electric vehicles, and other alternatives to carbon sequestration, are examples of how we can transition away from ethanol dependence over time. Unfortunately, the 2024 presidential election makes any shift less likely in the near future.

My point is that ethanol doesn't have to die for us to protect our soil and water—if we want to. In fact, you can argue our ability to continue producing crops to use for biofuels is the best reason to increase conservation efforts. Leading with the idea ethanol must die simply picks a fight we can't win, feeds opponents' claims there are enemies of agriculture, and in the grand scheme of things is poor political judgment. I can certainly be accused of exercising bad judgment, having on numerous occasions said the Iowa Farm Bureau is a corrosive force. Statements like this are provocative but not as provocative as saying ethanol must die.

Part of the challenge with ethanol and our swine production and corn growing system, is the fact they are currently the building blocks of Iowa agriculture and the main impacts on nature. They aren't going away, largely because they have strong and wide economic and political power. If we begin with the premise they must end or must change drastically, we have already lost the argument. The better question is, How do we harness their importance to argue that more must be done to change our systems if we want to protect our productive capacity? We are threatening the future of Iowa's farm economy by not caring for our soil and water today.

People involved in agriculture like to believe that being free from any form of regulations to protect soil and water is good policy. This is the premise of right to farm laws. However, our unwillingness to establish even basic standards of stewardship for soil and water threatens the very future of this promised freedom. Fertility declines, soil health degrades, water infiltration slows, all leading us to do things like applying even more fertilizer and installing more tile lines to address the side effects of an abusive farming system. As soil degrades, it contains less carbon and is more compact, meaning the water pools on the surface and then runs off. This type of drainage issue can't be corrected by putting in more drainage tile. The real answer lies with wiser farm practices and better soil health. Cover crops and more diversified crop rotations can improve soil quality, as can mixing in prairie strips on unproductive fields. Hogs are part of Iowa's history and future, but the key challenge is how we handle their manure. Today we do a poor job of managing manure, often failing to account for its crop nutrient value when applying it and not adequately preventing its negative effects on water quality. We treat manure as waste rather than as a valuable resource. This can change and needs to.

## THE REALITY OF AGRICULTURE'S RELATION TO NATURE

As January 2025 unfolded and the new administration took office, departing Secretary of Agriculture Tom Vilsack, in one of his final official statements, objected to the recent Environmental Protection Agency report to Congress on biofuels. He objected to EPA's conclusion that overall, production of biofuels including ethanol is marginally bad for the environment. Of course this set the secretary and biofuel supporters howling, claiming EPA was being unfair in its conclusion, especially given how important biofuels have been for the agricultural economy, farmers, and land values.

Concluding that biofuels have been negative for the environment should not come as a surprise. How is chemically intensive corn production not bad for soil conservation and water quality? Ethanol's supporters point to what they see as the environmental benefits of re-newable energy and reductions in greenhouse gases. The agricultural sector doesn't want to accept that on balance agriculture has a neg-ative effect on the environment. Ironically, the farm sector expends great efforts resisting many programs with the potential to make crop production less harmful. Attend any legislative hearing involving the environment and agriculture and I guarantee you will hear an Iowa farmer crow about how farmers are the first environmentalists and how no one cares more for the land and water. News flash—most ar-en't environmentalists, even if they've convinced themselves other-wise. That farmers love the environment is the carapace agriculture pulls into, hoping, like the turtle, to avoid any threats. This is a key part of our problem. In many ways it crystallizes the contradiction in our thinking about agriculture's relationship to nature and the envi-ronment. Observers like to believe it can be benign or even positive, but it isn't.

By design, agriculture is consumptive—think of water use—and abusive—think of land conversion and soil erosion—and polluting—consider water quality with fertilizer use and animal waste disposal. Most efforts relating to soil conservation and environmental laws for agriculture over the last 50 years have had the goal of making it less harmful to the natural world. This was the whole premise for devel-oping sustainable agriculture, what some now refer to as regenerative agriculture. It is seen in the evolving dreams many had for so-called Climate-smart agriculture—or at least had until Trump and the new USDA banished the term from the lexicon. Regardless of what you call it, most effects of agriculture on the environment have been—and are—negative. You can't till millions of acres of land, spread chemical fertilizers and animal wastes on it, douse it with pesticides, often several times a year, and leave it bare to nature's forces of rain and wind for over half the year—and then portray this as benign! Certainly we have made progress on soil conservation during the 90 years and billions of dollars we've invested in addressing it. Our progress on water quality has been much less, largely because we chose to legally exempt most agricultural practices polluting water from any form of control. Intensive crop production, especially our favorite form—rotating corn and soybean monocultures—are not environmentally beneficial. Even minimum tillage or no-till systems may not be less harmful, as these practices simply trade off heavier use of pesticides for reduced tillage.

When the EPA concludes biofuels, the economic darling of agriculture and the foundation for sustainable aviation fuel hopes, aren't positive for the environment, the agricultural sector could not accept this truth, conveniently overlooking the reality that most intensive crop production isn't either. My point is that environmental protection or enhancement has never been the goal of agriculture! Ever since we began plowing prairies and draining wetlands, farming has degraded nature. The goal of agriculture is growing food to create economic opportunities and profits for farmers, businesses, and rural communities. This is good for the nation, good for agriculture, and good for farmers but less good for nature and the environment. We justify farm program payments, crop insurance subsidies, the renewable fuel standard, and many other economic supports as benefiting farmers and society. They are also marginally bad for nature and the environment. Trying to make them less so is an important policy goal, but believing agriculture is a positive or even a nature-enhancing activity is magical thinking. We have to recognize that both conclusions are true rather than try to convince ourselves farming is environmentally beneficial. Trying to deny this reality distracts us from considering how the gap can be narrowed by using the knowledge we have for conserving soil and protecting water quality.

## Nature's Thoughts on Why We Seem Conflicted

All this raises several questions for me. Why don't more of you do these things, use the tools and knowledge you have to protect me? What is it with your attitude toward me and why the reluctance? I've thought about these questions and here are some possible answers. Look at the list and see if any describe your situation:

You just don't care.

You don't believe these things will actually work.

It is too much trouble or it is so much of a change from your normal routine that it isn't worth the effort.

Perhaps your concern is it costs too much, either in money or in time.

Maybe nature takes too long and won't yield immediate results, the instant gratification you crave in your busy lives.

It may seem too much like work, like a chore rather than being fun.

Perhaps it goes against your beliefs—you fear thinking more about me will somehow elevate me over other priorities, perhaps even conflict with your religious views and your God-given domination.

Perhaps it violates your politics or your ideology. Conservatives have effectively hung the "radical environmentalist label" on anyone who wants to do something positive for me, the environment, or climate change. Perhaps you worry believing in these ideas will reveal you are woke and going soft on your MAGA principles!

I don't mean to offend anyone by raising these ideas, but won't examining them help us discover why you may disregard me and help us identify ways to change your behavior? The point is you don't need to wait for your legislature or Congress or the courts to protect me. There are many things you can do, often in your own backyard and in your community, to benefit me— and your health. The point Louv, Tallamy, and many others in my tribe are making is new actions to support and show your love for me are most effective when they are personal and local. Doing any of these things will help me know that you are not one of nature's thieves.

## ACKNOWLEDGING THE GOOD SIDES OF IOWA FARMING

As someone who has worked in Iowa agriculture for over 40 years, I am well aware few people appreciate a critic, especially one willing to call out the foolishness and abuses often marking our agricultural thinking. If you read the land and river books you know this has not stopped me from raising issues we need to confront. Many will take offense at my observations about the ways our agricultural system harms nature. Challenging our willingness to believe we can produce our way out of our current circumstances through greater reliance on biofuels is not for the faint of heart. Daring to criticize agriculture makes it too easy for those who take offense to paint you as the enemy, as someone who hopes "modern agriculture" will come to a halt, someone unwilling to admit the good things about farming and Iowa's rural culture. My answer to that is there are healthier ways to grow our food.

As a child of Iowa's rural culture and as someone embedded in agriculture and food production all my life, I am well aware of the broad array of attitudes and approaches found among farmers, landowners, agricultural organizations, and officials. No one wakes up in the morning with the goal of making matters worse, polluting the water, eroding the soil, or abusing animals. But we know these things happen. Everyone who works the land is a student of nature, is engaged in its use and hopefully in its care. But it is obvious not everyone shares the same perspectives on the importance of nature, the risks our current practices pose, or the opportunities to use sound policy and the tools of justice to promote a more sustainable future.

In the Iowa agriculture community, one farm organization in particular deserves mention for the role it plays. Practical Farmers of Iowa was created over 40 years ago by a small group of family farmers guided by concerns of caring for the land and providing a future for their families and communities. To outside observers the founders could be portrayed as old-fashioned in their thinking, using traditional methods of crop rotations, growing small grains and pasture, integrating livestock into their farms, and caring more about how to survive profitably and happily rather than about purchasing the newest equipment or their neighbor's land. Over the years PFI has provided opportunities for farmers who appreciate the wisdom of traditional farming practices to coalesce under the theme of sustainable agriculture. This is not the same as organic farming, though it is embraced. The focus is not on chemically intensive methods, though chemicals are used when needed; instead the focus is, as the name states, on the practical.

Since 1985 PFI has grown into a robust organization with over 5,000 members, 30-plus staff, and a budget of $20 million a year. Some funding comes from government grants with over half used to provide cost-sharing assistance to member farmers employing conservation practices the organization promotes. As you might imagine, reliance on federal grants made the organization vulnerable to the slash and burden idiocy of the DOGE efforts of early 2025, but the organization has persevered. Perhaps its most edifying trait is the wide slate of field days it sponsors throughout the year. Field days take place mostly on participating farmers' land, offering education and practical advice across the range of agriculture. From tillage to weed control, from on-farm processing and direct marketing to land acquisition and farm succession planning, PFI members are involved in all dimensions of farming. "We use farmer led investigation and information sharing to help farmers practice an agriculture that benefits both land and people" is how the organization describes its work.

PFI's success comes in part from having charted a course largely free from political entanglements—selling insurance or fronting for corporations. It does not espouse the antigovernment, probusiness agenda reflected in the work of many farm groups, like the Iowa Farm Bureau. While its members most likely fall into the progressive camp, its diversity of membership includes all persuasions ranging from aging hippies to new farmers, from libertarians to Mennonites and all parts in between. All its members are drawn by the shared vision of "an Iowa with healthy soil, healthy food, clean air, clean water, resilient farms, and vibrant communities." As PFI's membership grows it reaches an increasing share of Iowa's farms and the success of their farming practices help demonstrate there are ways caring for the soil, water, and livestock can be profitable and sustainable. Their success of their efforts go to the very heart of concerns about who will be the next generation of Iowa farmers.

The Iowa Farmers Union (IFU) is a more traditional farm group with a history reaching back over 100 years. Its members share a progressive family orientation to farming and farm policy much like PFI. But as a state affiliate of the National Farmers Union, the IFU has had a much longer and more productive involvement in policy and legislative matters. In many ways the Farmers Union, at both the state and federal level, has played the role of being a political counter balance to the more conservative views of Farm Bureau and the commodity organizations. The political reality though is the IFU membership, while having doubled in recent years, is relatively small when compared to the Farm Bureau and many commodity organizations. Even so, most political observers would agree the IFU hits above its weight when it comes to political advocacy.

Both organizations have parallels in the work of Niman Ranch whose farmers use traditional methods to raise pigs, what modern ag folks call old-fashioned and inefficient. In its 30 years Niman Ranch has grown to serve over 700 family farms in Iowa and neighboring states. The sows are raised outside, farrowing the piglets the traditional way in individual huts. Most Niman pigs are fattened or finished in deeply bedded hoop houses, never confined to live crowded together above a cesspool of their own wastes; the pigs are bred to survive outdoors in fluctuating temperatures. Most importantly, the meat they produce tastes different. It tastes like pork. Chefs and shoppers across the nation who crave the delicious flavor of meat with fat and texture drive the market for Niman Ranch. Several years ago Niman Ranch was acquired by Perdue, a major national poultry company. Some feared the merger would mean the unique values of animal care and quality meat Niman Ranch was famous for might be lost. The good news is history has shown the merge has done much more to change the values and production practices used by Perdue than it has affected Niman.

The family farmers who sell pigs through Niman share several common features. Most would tell you if Niman Ranch didn't exist they would be out of swine production, in large part because they refuse to raise their animals any other way. Second, by honoring their work and their animals Niman Ranch has helped restore the joy in farming. This makes it possible for them to see a future for their farms and families. The average age of American farmers is nearly 60, while the average age of a Niman farmer is in the 40s. Many have the next generation anxious to return to the farm. The respect they show extends not just to the eaters and to their animals but also to the land, to nature. I mention Practical Farmers of Iowa, the Iowa Farmers Union, and Niman Ranch to make sure you know of their good work and to highlight the fact agriculture and farming do not need to be the enemy of nature or of the public's interest in a sustainable future. Our challenge is helping create more opportunities for farmers to marry their appreciation and love for nature with producing the food and fiber the nation needs.

You might think this all sounds well and good Professor, but it must be expensive or impossible to achieve these goals—otherwise why haven't we? The simple answer: doing this hasn't been a priority. Practices are available and are certainly not impossible or even difficult to implement. Consider this list of 15 things we could do to promote nature, improve conservation, and support better farming:

1) Plant cover crops and look for ways to graze them.

2) Install streamside buffer strips and prohibit farming up to the river edge.

86

3) Keep cows out of streams by fencing banks and controlling access.

4) Stop farming in the two-year floodplain, and don't offer crop insurance there.

5) End the common practice of fall tillage.

6) Set limits on the installation of new tile lines based on the water-handling capacity of the streams and ditches where the water is being drained.

7) Use the maximum return to nitrogen or MRTN rate when applying fertilizer.

8) Diversify crop production, restore grasslands, and return to producing the small grains much in demand, like the millions of acres of oats we once grew.

9) Use prairie strips where possible on unproductive land, using the continuous Conservation Reserve Program or CRP to improve pollinator and wildlife habitat.

10) Require nutrient management plans and focus on building soil health, increasing carbon content, and improving water infiltration rates.

11) Limit the fall application of anhydrous ammonia.

12) Use the USDA's conservation stewardship program or CSP to fund changes in farming practices on working lands.

13) Monitor and enforce compliance with manure management plans, and prohibit using the same fields for multiple applications in multiple plans.

14) Enforce the USDA's conservation compliance requirements.

15) Provide more funding for soil and water conservation districts to implement Iowa's soil protection laws and to develop farm and watershed conservation plans.

If nature is only an afterthought in how we farm then we shouldn't be surprised if our farming practices are harmful. But if we really want to reform agriculture and promote nature we have many ways to do this. Hundreds of Iowa farm families are employing these practices to make their farms more profitable and sustainable. We need thousands more to join them. By adopting these common sense practices we can improve the performance, both economically and environmentally, of our farming system.

# Chapter 5
# Chasing Climate Dollars: Agriculture's Next White Whale?

Arriving early for a meeting in Solon north of Iowa City gave me time to stroll the downtown. Near the intersection of Highway 1 and Main Street is a boulder placed in the 1930s by the Daughters of the American Revolution marking Dillon's Furrow. The marker shares a story about the path plowed in 1839 by Lyman Dillon under contract with the U.S. government, a tale elaborated on in *On the Trail of Lyman Dillon* by Douglas Monk. In March 1839 Congress appropriated $20,000 to set out a trail from Dubuque to the Missouri border to move dragoons and goods between the growing cities. The first portion of what became the military trail was between Dubuque and Iowa City, soon to become the territorial capital in 1841.

In what has become a well-trod path, the military entered into a contract with Dillon to plow a furrow between Dubuque and Iowa City marking the trail. He undertook the project in August 1839, essentially plowing a line between the eastern Iowa woodlands and the prairie stretching to the west. The legacy of Dillon's Furrow remains because much of Highway 1 follows Dillon's route. Traveling from Iowa City north at Solon, on to Mount Vernon, then Martelle, Anamosa, and Monticello, and on through Cascade you eventually reach Dubuque. All along this route you are traveling the furrow plowed by Lyman Dillon. As significant as his project was, details of how it was completed are in some doubt. Historians say he plowed using a team of 10 oxen, while modern observers believe there was no need for so many. Even the direction he followed is in question. Some say he plowed from Dubuque to Iowa City; others contend the path was reversed. Since he lived in Iowa City, it may be the logical starting point. In either case, there is no doubt the job was done, payment made, and the trail marked.

This process of marking the edges of our settlement, defining the start of the frontier, was repeated often in our history. What came next was also typically repeated: a flow of settlers, many who would use the frontier trail to push further west, forcing whoever or whatever was there to move. By the time of statehood in 1846, Dillon's Furrow marked what would become a highway, still in use today. As you consider our relation with nature issues of water quality, land stewardship, protecting endangered species, and addressing climate change in many ways mirror a continuation of Dillon's work. Drawing a line between two known points, then marking a frontier for the actions we hope will be possible in the years ahead, describes where we as a nation are in addressing climate issues. We know where we are, and many of us believe we know where we need to go, but the path forward is full of twists, turns, and obstacles, rendering the outcome of the journey uncertain.

## CLIMATE CHANGE: WHAT WAS NEW IS NOW FORBIDDEN

The American nature policy experiencing the most drastic and dramatic shift relates to efforts to integrate any concern for climate into natural resource policies on energy production, agriculture and food programs, and land management efforts. In recent years the nation has made significant progress, gaining more acceptance and understanding of the changing climate and our need to address it in government programs. The USDA played a leading role in these programs. In this chapter, my primary focus is the climate work of the Biden administration. My concern is we risked turning the efforts into simply a dollar chase, with examples such as sustainable aviation fuel and carbon sequestration. Even though some of the following discussion is critical, the efforts of the Biden administration differ in one major way from the climate policy of the new.

The simplest and most accurate way to describe the new administration's attitude is, *we don't believe it and we want no part of it.* As a result, literally billions of dollars of government funding have been put on hold, actually clawed back, reversed, or simply wasted. Hundreds of grants to universities, businesses, and other organizations as well as contractual agreements entered into with thousands of farmers and landowners have been summarily canceled or had funding withheld indefinitely. At this point, it is impossible to know if these radical actions will be upheld in the court challenges now underway, or if they may be reversed either because the administration comes to recognize some were foolish and unjustified, or because the courts reverse them as illegal, as is the early trend.

A final comment before turning to climate issues relates to the rule of law. As a lawyer and law professor, I've spent my career working with the tools of justice, the subject of chapter 9. The rule of law serves as both a polestar and the rock upon which the legislative and judicial systems are grounded. Our historic reliance on the rule of law has fostered a perhaps overconfident view that it couldn't be challenged.

This is what makes many recent actions by officials in the new administration, even those reportedly working for the Department of Justice, especially frightening. The lack of respect for the rule of law, for the judicial branch, for the separation of powers, and for the legitimate functions of the legislative branch to fund government and provide oversight of the executive branch are radical and dangerous shifts in America's policy—not just for our nation and citizens but for the institution of justice itself and its role as the bulwark for democracy. Nature has told us that it takes the long look, good advice for us as well. The new administration and the warped view of governing it embraces are threats, but they too will pass. When they do nature will still be here to offer solace, and if we fight for them, law and democracy will still be here too.

## Nature on Turning Climate Concerns into a Dollar Chase

The professor promised me this is a hopeful book and it is, I have read to the end. This is why I am excited to contribute thoughts on this chapter, your responses to climate change. I originally hoped your actions held promise for our forging a healthier working relation, one benefiting me—nature—and benefiting you, your climate, and your quality of life. Having looked a little closer at your plans, I have to apologize for what may sound like a somewhat sour note to kick this off. Unfortunately, as the professor just explained, the sour note is being supplemented by one even more bitter coming from the antiscience, antinature ideology of the new administration. My advice for now is to ignore them as best you can.

It was comforting for me to see you finally becoming concerned about the impact your actions have on influencing the climate and me. The enthusiastic response the agricultural business sector showed to the climate issue was impressive. You Americans are so imbued with the entrepreneurial spirit! The Carbon Cowboys such as Indigo Ag, who in recent years promoted carbon contracting to farmers are now being joined by a new wave of pioneers, many working on the frontier of sustainable aviation fuel. (The new people in charge have proposed changing the label to synthetic aviation fuel apparently because "sustainable" is too woke.) One can only hope some good will come from this activity. You don't need another draft of companies created to farm the farmers; plenty of those already exist. Excuse my metaphor, but my worry is these climate developments are not new wine in new bottles, but just the same stale brew of promises and plans, warmed over and served up to farmers with new graphics, formatting, and claims—lots of sizzle leading to an eventual fizzle. As you like to say, time will tell—and I have plenty of it.

I had hoped this might be an opportunity for you to demonstrate the wisdom of how working with nature can lead to more productive and sustainable systems. Instead, it appears many of you may only see this as a money chase, an opportunity to roll out new technologies, elaborate schemes, and promises of riches to farmers. Your modern approach for dealing with the climate is to offer up a tantalizing array of new opportunities for those wise enough to jump on board early, then hope good things result.

Let's start by looking at the two candidates racing out of the starting block and how they illustrate my concerns. First is the Summit Carbon Solutions proposal to build a 2,500-mile pipeline network to carry compressed $CO_2$ in liquid form. The $CO_2$ will be collected from ethanol plants and fertilizer factories in Iowa and neighboring states. The second is sustainable aviation fuel the "new" product promoters portray as the future of agriculture. Excuse me if I don't see these "promising opportunities" as particularly wise or helpful in dealing with the climate. They do, however, share a number of similarities:

First, they involve expensive, complicated infrastructure, requiring millions in investments. Second, they are being created and offered to farmers mainly by outsiders, new industries and companies not traditionally involved with farming. Third, both involve relatively complex legal and contractual arrangements for participating farmers and businesses; some even require raising new crops. Fourth, they are premised on the claim that agriculture can survive and farmers can keep doing what they love, especially growing corn, only by signing on to the new approaches. Fifth, they assume my active compliance—a benevolent nature, offering plenty of soil, water, land, and energy to make the systems go—no questions asked. Sixth, the new miracle cures promise to yield enough profits to make the promoters rich and the farmers happy.

The icing on the cake is that by getting on board now, farmers and agricultural businesses can address the pesky fears some have about climate change without really having to change their ways. This is what you call a win-win-win approach. So much winning! Here is my cautionary note: You can fool yourselves but you can't fool Mother Nature.

You might think I'm being a little unfair in my characterization, so let me give you an illustration. Take the company Farmonaut, an Indianapolis-based satellite company trying to establish a footprint in the sustainable aviation fuel market. It hopes to do so largely through promoting new oilseed crops, such as mustard, canola, and sunflower. According to the website, its "satellite based farm management solutions are helping farmers make data-driven decisions to maximize their yields while maintaining sustainability." The website explains the key technologies being employed: precision agriculture, AI-driven crop health monitoring, block chain-based traceability, and advanced weather forecasting. It appears the only technology not mentioned is Bitcoin, but no doubt you can enroll using it.

When you look at this description, isn't it fair to conclude that it is primarily about selling the technology of the new platform? There is hardly any mention of the production challenges, the costs of harvesting, the marketing issues and other traditional farming concerns, especially when raising new crops. The company claims many important environmental benefits will result: reducing the carbon footprint of agriculture, improving soil health through crop rotations and diversification, decreased use of harmful fertilizers and pesticides, enhanced biodiversity in the agricultural landscape, and reduced water consumption. Now these are all important environmental benefits, but don't they sound familiar? Aren't these the same goals claimed by those promoting regenerative agriculture? All these benefits are available using existing agriculture technologies, obtained by relying on sustainable practices and good farming, not satellites and block chain.

The ideas of sustainable aviation fuel and $CO_2$ pipelines may be parables for what is wrong with modern agriculture. Climate-smart agriculture risks becoming a chase for dollars, obscuring common sense and the traditional role of public agencies, extension, and law in promoting the public good. Instead the new goals appear to be privatize it, commodify it, support it with artificial markets, then prop it up if necessary with public funding and tax credits—all to create new technologies to be marketed to farmers. Plus at the end of the day you can still call it sustainable! Enough of my rant, time for the Professor to take over.

# CLIMATE-SMART COMMODITIES: NEW VISION FOR AGRICULTURE OR EPHEMERAL DREAM?

You have just read how Climate-smart agriculture will be used to produce Climate-smart commodities. These concepts were all the rage among some audiences in rural America, at least before January 21, 2025, who believe coming to grips with the impacts of a changing climate means that agriculture must play a leading role. In some ways this is symptomatic of our modern approach to conservation and politics. The first step is a well-intended idea. Here it is, our eventual need to address climate issues and engage farmers and agricultural businesses in this critical work. The best way to do so is to use market-based, or at least market-like, incentives to promote it. We insist on using markets because we are familiar with how they work and are wedded to the conviction that all efforts must be entirely voluntary rather than regulatory. However, because markets don't exist for most of the Climate-smart goods or services envisioned, the actual money to make this work will need to come from the public, that is, taxpayers, through direct payments, tax incentives, or a combination, at least until such time as real markets can develop, if ever. This is the second step, using public subsidies to try to induce changes in social behavior, hoping the economy will adjust.

The third step is the need for a good name to describe this new opportunity, a label to capture the imagination and innovation involved. In this case the term of choice is Climate-smart commodities. This is a gem because it captures all the elements: it deals with climate, it is a subtle way to throw shade on existing programs, and it focuses on commodities, something we can see, feel, measure, and value. The search for an effective label to identify more enlightened approaches to farming has a rich history. It was conservation farming in the mid-20th century. Then sustainable agriculture emerged in the 1980s as a broader, more encompassing term than organic farming. By the turn of this century the shine was wearing off sustainability, in part because its malleability and expansive nature allowed the term to be slapped on nearly any agricultural practice or product. The effect was to lose its power and meaning. This has led to current interest, some might say a groundswell of interest, in the new label, the sexy term regenerative agriculture. It sounds great—who can argue with the idea? And it can easily serve as a rallying point because it offers imagination, inspiration, and hope. The fact that its exact meaning is uncertain and often in the eye of the beholder or practitioner is problematic, but this has not diminished interest in its use. Only time will tell if the term can be defined in ways to make its promise real and give it the strength to bear the weight of the expectations being loaded onto it. Maybe we can read it to include "Climate-smart." For good measure, perhaps the new regime can harness the term to support the MAHA agenda to make America healthy again!

Now we come to the fourth step in this process, the rollout or implementation. For Climate-smart commodities this was entirely driven by the Biden-Vilsack USDA with several billions of dollars allocated to the effort. The funding came largely from the oddly named Inflation Reduction Act of 2023. Using the funds and his relatively unhindered administrative power, Secretary Vilsack quickly developed and put in the field a generous federal grant program to support farmers, farm groups, businesses, and universities arrayed and combined however they saw fit. The program was originally to spend $2 billion, but the popularity and number of applicants led the secretary to unilaterally add an additional

$1 billion in funding. Even with a fairly tight deadline and a complicated application process, hundreds of proposals were submitted. By early 2023 the USDA had selected more than 140 projects to fund, involving over 500 nonprofits and for-profit businesses as well as 100 universities. The project plans involve 14,000 farms and 3 million acres of land. The success of the USDA in implementing the grant program and getting the money out the door (allegedly) can only be described as impressive, a win for those who believed the initiative offered a real opportunity for change on climate and in agriculture.

Realistically these hopes may prove to be overly optimistic. The real test will be when recipients implement the activities promised in the proposals. For most grantees the first year was spent completing the burdensome paperwork to get contracts entered and signed by the USDA. Because this grant, like most USDA grants, operates on a reimbursement basis, grantees need to use their own funds or those from their required match from partners, to actually initiate any work.

As you might have guessed, it is at this point the politics of the new administration intruded into the process, with "official" USDA actions to cancel all Climate-smart agreements, refusing to reimburse farmers and grant recipients for money already spent. In other words, this is a real apple cart turnover with serious legal and financial implications for all involved—issues soon to be sorted out in the courts.

Leaving aside for the time being this uncertainty, what are the early returns? As you might imagine, it is too soon to tell. Can the public expect a return on the funds in positive climate impacts and new profitable ventures for farmers and agriculture? Certainly the promises made in the applications indicate this is possible. Many positive changes were proposed and many interesting, innovative initiatives were suggested. Projects often involve tried and tested conservation farming practices with positive climate impacts, like using cover crops, manure digesters for energy production, and better fertilizer practices to protect water quality. Here is the real question and test for the future of Climate-smart commodities, however—do they really exist? Will truly transformative changes result or is the label just a new descriptor that echoes nature's concern about putting old wine in new bottles? Listen closely when something is described as Climate-smart and ask whether the commodities being produced would not otherwise exist.

All this supposes the initiative even survives in the new political era, one marked not just by hostility to anything labeled climate or created by the Biden administration or by new efforts to cut "wasteful" government spending. The DOGE effort is sure to look askance at anything as identified with the previous administration as part of the Climate-smart commodity program. The first months of the new administration raise serious questions about the program's continued existence, increasing the likelihood the dollars will be clawed back or denied. If this happens, organizations hiring staff to implement the projects and spending funds they expected to receive will face significant hardships. As disruptive as this may be, it could be a chance to return to first principles. Perhaps agriculture can find a new label like common sense good farming—based on doing things we know work and have had available for years, but approaches we just resisted using.

## How Markets Work

One benefit of growing up in the U.S. capitalist economy is by the time you turn seven you have a broad understanding of how markets work. This may seem fairly obvious, but it is valuable if you ever have to work with people who grew up in nonmarket economies like Cuba or former Soviet states. As a 7 year-old collecting my allowance or earning pocket money doing farm chores, I understood the five elements required for a market to function. I was the buyer. The product was baseball cards. The Topps company made them, conveniently packaged with gum. Woolsworths in Lenox sold them at the affordable price of 25¢ a pack. It was all there—buyer, seller, product, market, and value. The story is no different today. If I want to buy a bottle of bourbon, I can visit my friend and former student Jamie Walters, one of my Rabbit Lake companions, at Whiskey Acres near DeKalb. He sells it at the farm for a price he sets per bottle in dollars, which I happen to have—buyer, seller, product, market, value—all five elements are there.

Why explain this basic process to you? Because many people in modern agriculture want to believe it is possible to protect and enhance nature; deal with such challenging issues as improving water quality, protecting soil health, and addressing climate change; and even create new income and profits for farmers all at the same time by marketing ecosystem services. Sustainable aviation fuel, as nature has described, is an example of one such service. The main problem for many examples of ecosystem services, including sustainable aviation fuel is most, if not all, of the elements required to have a market are missing.

Don't get me wrong: nature can and does produce an array of invaluable services—they make our survival possible! Harnessing soil fertility, sunlight, and rain to grow food; cycling nutrients through the soil to food, to us and then back; cycling rain from the rivers to the oceans and back—you get the picture. All the uses of nature we harness—food, fiber, energy—are ecosystem services, ones we often purchase through the marketplace.

The new idea people who discuss ecosystem services refer to is an effort to broaden the concept of products, to try to harness market forces to pay for things we either don't need to purchase—like expecting clean water—or an identifiable product we don't have—such as the concept of regenerative agriculture. These services are instead what you might consider to be public goods. As citizens we expect our water to not be polluted. As regular eaters we expect soils to not be eroded so farmers can continue producing food. Our ability to expect or assume these will exist is a function of market signals and the legal system. We pay money for food so that farmers and companies will produce it. Laws are in place to promote soil conservation and protect water quality. To the extent the laws place costs on people, in a market economy, these costs are passed to consumers in the higher prices we pay.

Now it is true markets are not perfect and there can be many costs associated with producing goods not reflected in the market price. For example, the low pay given to farm laborers may help keep food prices low, but the effects of under paying workers are passed on to society in social costs like their health care. The pollution that Iowa puts into our rivers affects communities downstream. This is a moral hazard with the costs borne by others. These are what economists refer to as externalities, costs not reflected in the market price of products. Here again is where laws may step in. Requiring a factory to address water quality means the "extra" costs will be charged in the market rather than imposed on those downstream drinking dirty water. To the extent that laws or regulations are not used to address externalities, as with most farm-based pollution, resources are depleted, and social costs are created and passed to others. One problem faced by farmers producing commodities and not products (like Jamie's bourbon) is they are price takers rather than price setters. This makes it difficult to pass higher costs on to consumers. One way to address this is to use eco-labels on food products that describe their unique traits—think of cage-free eggs. Consumers who desire these products will pay more so farmers can be paid more for their actions. Ecosystem services are a form of eco-labeling, but the social benefits produced are not usually identifiable products.

As a nation founded on a market economy, we are naturally attracted to using markets to improve our lives. We experience this reality every day as new technologies and products appear and as items we never thought of a few years ago become indispensable, like your cell phone and my computer. It is a shared American dream to invent a new product, develop a technology, or otherwise tap into the stream of commerce to reap the economic rewards. It is why we believe in higher education and offer patents to protect intellectual property.

You may be wondering, how does this relate to ecosystem services and nature? It is a critical recognition to understand that most of the ecosystem services provided by nature are not new! Clean water is not like a cell phone. It is not a new idea and it is not clear how it can be "improved"—clean water is clean water! Instead it just needs to exist, to be protected and respected by the actors in our economy, especially those whose activities can degrade it. This requires using the power of law and regulation, as well as public education and subsidies where necessary, to help provide it—not just markets. Producing food, growing grains in ways to sustain the soil and improve its health, and not polluting the water are not new ideas. These have been the direct goal of federal policies for almost 90 years and are—or should be—the primary goals of farming. The problem is even with this long history we still struggle to achieve these objectives—to protect soil, preserve land, enhance soil health, and not degrade our water.

So then what is new? At least two things are new. One is what we are talking about, why many people latch on to ecosystem services as the answer to move us forward. The theory is that by harnessing markets, farmer resistance to achieving nature goals will wane and the public will be rewarded. In other words, the premise is that we have just been going about it wrong by trying to use education and laws rather than economics to influence behavior. The second new thing, or at least current aspect, is the challenge of climate change. We recognize that the climate is changing, largely due to our activities, and if we want to change directions, we need to change our ways.

## THE RECIPE FOR A BOONDOGGLE: WHO WANTS TO BUY SOME CARBON?

Webster's defines *boondoggle* as "a wasteful or impractical project or activity often involving graft." If you are interested in mixing up a good old-fashioned boondoggle, here are the ingredients you need:

A billionaire scheme to get rich off public subsidies.

Politicians fixated on climate issues, trying to support large-scale solutions, using tax credits, that is, free money, to encourage behavior changes.

A state's addiction to growing corn and producing ethanol to support the habit.

Feckless politicians of both stripes, at the federal and state level, happy to help friends and donors make money and wanting to show progress on climate issues.

A one-sided administrative process: slanted to approving new utility projects, with little public involvement, with power to grant eminent domain to private businesses over objections of opposing landowners.

Mix well, then spread into a pan, well greased with political contributions, and sprinkle with high-paid lawyers and political connections.

This is the Summit Carbon Solutions Co2 pipeline project now roiling the economy and political landscape of Iowa. All the ingredients are there—except for the graft, or so we assume. The irony—it is based on nonmarket-created public economic supports from climate-related government policies and generous federal tax credits, all subject to change. The three legs under the stool are the Renewable Fuel Standard, the Inflation Reduction Act 45Z tax credits for carbon sequestration, and California and Oregon's low carbon fuel programs. All promise to increase the value of ethanol and prolong its life.

What if I want to sell you a ton of carbon? Would it pique your interest? You might wonder what you would do with a ton of carbon and how much will it cost, assuming you are interested. How do we come up with a value so you know what to pay? Why consider doing something so unusual? These are good questions, but we are a little late asking them!

You may be surprised to learn we—the public—may already be on the hook to buy millions of tons of carbon at up to $85 a ton! At least we were. Time will tell if the new administration carries through with the plans. How did this come about and when did we agree to such a crazy idea? We really weren't involved in the decisions—instead it was Democrats in Congress and the Biden administration, passing the Inflation Reduction Act in summer 2023. The carbon portion was a small part of an omnibus bill costing hundreds of billions. It was intended to show by sequestering Co2, the U.S. could say it was finally doing something to address climate concerns. That should make you feel better. Now you may be wondering how does this relate to the pipeline?

Imagine this conversation between the public (P) and the pipeline promoters (CO).

CO—Have we got a deal for you! We promise to extend the market for ethanol and even increase its value. Doesn't that sound pretty attractive—think what it will do for the price of corn, land values, and tractor sales!

P—Wow, that does sound great, what do I need to do?

CO—Well, to begin you'll need to buy several million tons of compressed liquid Co2 from me at a price of up to $85 a ton. Don't worry, this won't actually cost any money out of pocket; instead it will be paid for with tax credits, meaning money you won't collect in the future.

P—Okay, but what am I going to do with all of that Co2?

CO—No worries—we are going to build a pipeline and pump it to North Dakota where it will be buried 5,000 feet underground. None of us will ever hear from it again, hopefully.

P—Is there catch?

CO—Well, you will have to repay us several billion dollars for burying the pipeline 2,500 miles and for constructing dozens of compression stations to condense the $CO_2$ gas into liquid. Then there is acquiring rights-of-ways across thousands of farm fields and buying easements from several thousand landowners. We (you) will need to pay hundreds of millions to get them to agree. Plus many will refuse to sell, requiring us to go through complicated eminent domain court proceedings. Otherwise it is a cinch.

P—Is there anything else we should know about possible risks?

CO—The generous federal tax credits to pay for the carbon and build the facility are already in federal law. Plus the extra value for the low carbon fuel premium we hope to receive is a feature of California and Oregon state law. And the market for ethanol depends on Congress continuing to support the Renewable Fuel Standard. Any of these could change, but we are optimistic that won't happen. Otherwise, those are all the risks—we believe it is still a cinch. Especially if we figure out how to get around the new South Dakota law prohibiting us from using eminent domain.

This is essentially what Summit Carbon Solutions proposed and Iowa utility officials approved, with the support of politicians and farmers.

So is the Co2 pipeline a boondoggle? This is a question you will need to answer yourself. My opinion is it is a bad idea. I will try to make this short and sweet.

First, the technology for $CO_2$ pipelines is new and largely untested at this scale. Many landowners along the corridor believe there are inherent risks transporting $CO_2$ in compressed liquid form. The concerns in part stem from an incident in Mississippi where a $CO_2$ pipeline ruptured, spreading poisonous gas across a wide area. Pipeline safety is why federal authorities regulating hazardous pipelines in early 2025 were poised to issue new safety guidelines. Many pipeline concerns relate to safety, but not all; however, under federal law, safety issues are under federal control. Pipeline promoters have tried using safety concerns as a universal solvent to wash away other state and local objections to locating and operating the pipeline, such as county zoning. By way of full disclosure, I was an expert witness for several counties in the Iowa Utility Board hearing, arguing the applicant refused to comply with county zoning. Utility officials rejected the argument, as have the federal courts.

Second the $CO_2$ pipeline is premised on addressing the climate, but even pipeline representatives acknowledge the $CO_2$ sequestered, although millions of tons, will have a negligible impact on improving the climate. This environmental reality did not prevent Congress and the Biden administration from green-lighting projects like $CO_2$ sequestration and offering generous 45Z federal tax credits. The goal appeared to be claiming to be doing something, even if there is little noticeable impact on our climate future.

Third supporters argue unless the technology is adopted, Iowa will lose the ethanol industry and the economic opportunities it creates. Iowa currently produces 25% of the nation's corn-based biofuels, so this threat gets attention. The argument is sequestering carbon will lower the carbon intensity score of Iowa ethanol, opening access to price premiums, such as the California low carbon initiative. The claim Iowa's ethanol industry is in jeopardy if $CO_2$ capture technology isn't developed is dubious. Claiming other states will quickly develop and invest billions of dollars to create a competitive biofuels sector ignores the reality Iowa already has over 40 ethanol plants with millions of gallons of capacity and the available corn supply to produce it.

Fourth once the $CO_2$ reaches North Dakota it may be used in advanced oil recovery, aka fracking, a process raising significant environmental issues. The strong resistance of landowners along the corridor, many of them corn growers, is further evidence the pipeline is questionable. They are not interested in having a pipeline buried in their land (over their objections), disrupting drainage systems, causing future productivity losses, and raising safety issues, even with the promised economic benefits.

Pipeline promoters expected little opposition given their claims the technology is essential to ethanol's future. State leaders, especially those enjoying campaign contributions from pipeline promoters and even employment, were happy to accept the arguments, but others who you might predict would be in favor resisted. The pipeline controversy even created unusual bedfellows when the Iowa Sierra Club and the Iowa Farm Bureau Federation joined to oppose aspects of the project. The Sierra Club, in particular through the work of Jess Mazour and Wally Taylor, has been the tip of the spear organizing Iowa landowner resistance. Dozens of rural Iowa legislators, many of them conservative Republicans, joined the opposition and are leading efforts to change Iowa law to prohibit private entities like Summit from using eminent domain. In the latest twist in early May of 2025 Republican Senators refused to vote on the required state budget until the House passed legislation to ban using eminent domain for $CO_2$ pipelines was brought to the Senate floor for a vote. After a lengthy and bitter floor debate the law was passed 27 to 22 and sent on to the governor for her possible signature. While passage of H.F. 639 gave the pipeline opponents cause to celebrate, their joy didn't last for long. In early June, in an action many political observers had predicted, Governor Reynolds vetoed the law claiming it would cause more damage to Iowa's economy than necessary. Her action opened a bitter wedge within the Iowa Republicans, with Speaker of the House Pat Grassley leading an effort to call the House back for a special session to over-ride the veto. While this action might happen, given the fact a 2/3 vote is required for an over-ride and the Senate vote was only 27-22, there is little reason to believe the Senate will support such an action. As a result the bitter divide and tensions caused by the eminent domain controversy will continue to fester and infect the 2026 election cycle.

Any profits (if they can be called that) resulting from the pipeline and sequestering the $CO_2$ will come from the public treasury rather than the marketplace. The "profits" exist almost exclusively in the form of lucrative federal tax credits, the 45Z program. The pipeline to carry the $CO_2$ liquid doesn't serve a market; instead it is a pipeline to federal subsidies. Creating what might appear to some to be a market, is essentially a magic trick. A wealth transfer between the public in the form of forgone federal tax revenues and financial benefits transferred to the pipeline owners. The sums in question may exceed $10 billion, thus the push!

Finally, most of the climate gains created by improving the performance of agriculture through carbon sequestration can be obtained much easier and more directly by changing farming practices. We could use farm-based local initiatives to go further down the climate road at a fraction of the cost. Instead, our plan is build a Rube Goldberg-like apparatus for gathering the $CO_2$, using huge quantities of energy to compress it and millions of gallons of water to cool the compressors, then pumping the liquid through 2,500 miles of pipeline buried across thousands of farms at the cost of several billion dollars, only to pump it 5,000 feet down in North Dakota,.

The Iowa utility authorities approved the permit for the pipeline in 2023, including the use of eminent domain. However, the Iowa permit is conditioned on construction not beginning until the project is approved in North and South Dakota. The expectation is that North Dakota will eventually approve it, but the story in South Dakota is much different. In the 2024 legislative session, South Dakota legislators debated a law to restrict use of eminent domain, but the effort failed. Supporters of the law, especially landowners along the route opposed to their land being taken, organized a powerful political movement resulting in the defeat in the November 2024 elections of many legislators who opposed the law. When the legislature met in early 2025, it quickly passed a law prohibiting the use of eminent domain by private pipelines, and the law was signed by the newly elected governor, a strong property rights advocate. As a result the pipeline has met a serious new roadblock. Its promoters asked South Dakota regulators to place an indefinite hold on considering their application but this request was denied and the application rejected for a second time. The ball is now back in Summit's court.

## SUSTAINABLE AVIATION FUEL: CHASING THE MYSTERIOUS MONEY

As 2025 began, perhaps the most important issue for many in agriculture—other than the changing administrations and the lack of a new farm bill—was the future of sustainable aviation fuel (SAF). The idea is relatively straight-forward: Use biofuels such as corn-based ethanol or diesel produced from oilseeds to make aviation fuel. Depending on how the fuel stocks are produced and the accounting method used, claims can be made the fuels have a lower carbon intensity. This means the aviation industry can use them to help claim reduced contributions to climate-warming greenhouse gas production. The challenges are how to develop and implement such a program and where to find the money to pay for it.

In January 2025, the USDA issued what it called "technical guidelines for claiming Climate-smart agriculture crops used as biofuel feedstock. The guidelines were intended to provide information on the potential mechanisms for producing the crops for the purpose of claiming the lucrative 45Z federal tax credits made available by the Inflation Reduction Act. The companies formed to pursue the money see sustainable aviation fuel as a way to unlock generous funds, perhaps even to provide farmers with additional income. The now former secretary of agriculture went so far as to claim that under the right circumstances crop producers in Illinois could earn as much as an extra dollar a bushel for corn produced according to the guidelines.

It is understandable people want to believe there is some new lucrative market waiting for them, if only they can find the key to unlock the storeroom. Last decade it was hemp and the decade before it was "pfarming"—raising bioengineered crops to produce drugs. Both proved to be flops as has using corn stalks to produce cellulosic ethanol. Sustainable aviation fuel may well fit into this category too. Sustainable aviation fuel has all the makings of being a white whale—an idea occupying the imaginations, energy, and bandwidth of many in agriculture. Whether it will actually produce new income or profits for farmers is uncertain and, from my perspective, largely in doubt. I may be wrong, and if so I will be the first to admit it when the day comes—assuming I live that long.

For now, it is worth examining the proposed mechanism the USDA suggested for implementing SAF in the technical guidelines. The following discussion is in the form of a theatrical playbill, introducing us to the characters and setting out the plot. The name of the mystery is *Follow the Money: Will Sustainable Aviation Fuel Make Farmers Profits?* I have to warn you the plot is a little complex and you might be left wondering if it is a mystery or a farce!

Here is the synopsis. Envision a future when farmers use environmentally beneficial practices to grow corn, soybeans, and sorghum and sell the crops produced using those practices to makers of biofuels. The biofuels are marketed to the aviation industry to fly the public and to claim significant reductions in the carbon intensity or greenhouse gases produced using the fuels. In exchange someone, most likely the public, pays for this behavior, through generous tax credits designed to encourage it or through higher ticket prices—and the climate is saved.

The cast and basic definitions so you can understand the action.

SAF—sustainable aviation fuel, the Holy Grail in the story.

CSA—Climate-smart agriculture, a suite of farming practices such as planting cover crops, using reduced tillage, and limiting fertilizer applications. The premise is these Climate-smart practices will result in crops with reduced carbon intensity.

Red CI—Reduced carbon intensity, a measure of how much less carbon is produced using these practices compared to conventionally grown crops.

The USDA included additional terms, the secondary characters we meet in various scenes. Here is a cheat sheet so the new acronyms are at hand.

BFR—the biofuel feedstocks report, a document created by the farmer for each crop being sold with an associated claim of Red CI.

FPA—farmer producer attestation, a document the farmer signs stating the number of bushels of crops produced on each farm field and the calculated Red CI.

FPOA—first point of aggregation, the party to whom the farmer

112

sells the crops produced using CSA, such as a biofuel producer or an intermediary.

TPV—the third party verifier, whom all FPOAs must employ to conduct audits on their records and audit a sample of farms and FPAs received from farmers.

TSGRPE—time stamped geo-referenced photographic evidence, the type of records farmers must keep if using the CSA practice of planting cover crops to demonstrate the biomass actually grown.

Mass balance approach—the accounting method used by biofuel producers, allowing them to comingle conventionally grown crops with those produced using CSA. Biofuel producers do not have to segregate CSA crops from conventionally grown crops, meaning any measure of claimed Red CI will be a percentage.

FD CIC—the feedstock carbon intensity calculator, a process developed by the USDA to allow producers to identify and calculate possible reductions in carbon intensity for crops produced using various forms of CSA on any field.

Now for the program.

Scene One - The farmer uses CSA on fields to produce crops with Red CI. The farmer keeps records for all the practices used on all fields, as well as the quantity harvested from each field, CSA and conventional. For each crop the farmer calculates the Red CI.

Scene Two - The farmer sells Red CI crops to the FPOA. The farmer provides the FPOA with copies of the BFR and the FPA relating to each crop, with the records identified by field and crop, so the FPOA can use the mass balance approach to calculate the Red CI of any biofuels produced using these crops.

Scene Three - Enter the TPV, hired by the FPOA and the biofuels producer, responsible for auditing both the FPOA's records and a sample of records from farms selling Red CI crops. The TPV visits the farms identified in the sample, the number sampled based on the square root of farms selling reduced CI crops to the FPOA. During the farm visit, the TPV reviews all records the farmer prepares (and retains for five years) to verify that the biofuel feed stocks and used in producing the SAF were actually raised using CSA. This certification holds the key to unlocking any treasures found in Scene Four.

Scene Four - The mystery of the money. The FPOA sells the Red CI SAF to an aviation company. At this point the play ends in mystery with the question of its resolution up in the air, no pun intended. Where will any money come from to pay the farmer for using the CSA or pay the FPOA for the costs of hiring the TPV? Will the FPOA pay the farmer a premium for raising the Red CI crops?

The audience is left wondering—who will provide the money? Might it be the aviation companies who buy the SAF and are entitled to receive 45Z federal tax credits? As the curtain falls the audience is encouraged to stay tuned for news of how this is resolved in the years ahead. Fade out. You, my friends, can decide if the play described is a mystery, a cliffhanger, or a farce. You might also wonder if most farmers will find these paper work requirements and record keeping obligations worth the candle? This is especially true when you compare this complicated process to the current two-step marketing system: grow corn—sell corn!

## Agriculture's Search for the Next White Whale

You are at it again, chanting your new mantra—all the buzz—of sustainable aviation fuel. The idea is you can take old-fashioned biofuels, think ethanol from corn or biodiesel from soybeans (and perhaps other crops), and through the magic of policy make them fuels the aviation sector will use to help the flying industry reduce its contributions to climate change and lower greenhouse gas emissions. The idea sounds great, achieving two goals at once, more profits and more demand for biofuels, helping keep the dinosaur afloat and giving the aviation sector the opportunity to don a green halo by saving the environment and boosting farm incomes. That is what you folks call a win-win scenario, a synergistic marvel.

This is so like you. When you are unable or unwilling to accomplish a goal you have set, often involving me—such as protecting water quality from pollution by fertilizer use—your answer is to move the goal lines or change the conversation to focus on a new shiny idea sure to address your needs. It often seems the need is more to convince yourselves you are making progress than really doing what needs to be done. The only problem with the idea of sustainable aviation fuel, at least from my perspective as nature, is its potential to be nothing more than a house of cards, one offering little in the way of real improvement for the climate or society. Instead, it offers a new crop of companies a window to sell technologies and promises to farmers on the premise they are doing the right thing. All will be underwritten or paid for with public money, largely through tax subsidies. By the time it becomes apparent the idea isn't going to pan out quite as you had hoped, or the complexity is such that farmers are not interested, you will no doubt have moved on to your next new idea. In other words, the promise of sustainable aviation fuel may be nothing more than agriculture pursuing its latest white whale.

## FACING THE FUTURE: ENERGY, A BETTER CLIMATE AND MORE

Ideas like carbon sequestration and sustainable aviation fuel, though open to the criticisms you have read, may play important roles in the nation's future. The key is our need to harness them in ways that make sense and complement thoughtful and systemic efforts to address the role of energy, development, and growth in society. Some argue the future depends on us shifting to the concept of degrowth to release ourselves from our belief that growth is always the answer. To them doing so is the only way to deal with the climate and many related issues. The adjustments such an approach would require in society combine to render it not just radical and high unlikely but, to my thinking, nonsensical in its rejection of the history of human progress. The good news is many policymakers, futurists, inventors, humanists, and others are striving to identify how society can address the challenges we face. If you are interested, the recent book *Abundance* by Ezra Klein and Derek Thompson weaves together many strands of this work, making it a valuable place to start and a vehicle for finding optimism for our future. Their central premise is in recent years much of the progressive agenda, such as reflected in the environmental movement, has devolved into a process largely marked by procedural steps presenting obstacles for taking action. As a result major infrastructure projects, such as high-speed rail, face lengthy delays and burgeoning costs, creating a reality where it seems government can not meet the needs of the public. The effect was to feed the antagonism toward public works and to limit the ability of the nation to actually utilize our talents and resources to achieve important goals. The authors present a strong case for how these trends can be reversed.

# Chapter 6
# Nature, Elections, and Politics: Did We Vote for Nature?

One challenge to writing a book about contemporary society is events keep happening after the writing stops, making it difficult to address or predict issues readily apparent to readers months later. This challenge is particularly heightened by our radically shifting political environment. The impact of the 2024 presidential election on policies and laws relating to nature has already been significant. The extent of the policy changes still unfolding is making it impossible to predict what conditions on the ground may be in the months ahead. Rather than ignore the changes, to act in good faith, I have attempted to address what is known and make reasonable predictions about what may come. Given the unprecedented chaos and ill-conceived rewiring of the federal government being inflicted on the nation, the difficulty is knowing how to address what is happening. I wrote much of this book in 2024—in what now seem to be relatively normal times. The final writing in June 2025 took place against the backdrop of new pronouncements with more expected to come.

My feelings about the current occupant of the White House were clearly stated in *The River Knows*. My hope was the nation would not just survive but would learn important lessons from his first term and, as a result, would avoid a second round of his madness. To my surprise and for the tens of million other citizens who shared my hope, this was not the case. Now the nation is facing a period of great risk and uncertainty. Much of the uncertainty is being played out in rapidly evolving actions attacking the traditional functions of government: staffing and funding of agencies and fulfilling governmental commitments in research grants and program contracts. While the impacts are being experienced across most parts of government, society and the economy, I am focusing on policies relating to nature, in particular questions of environmental law, public land, agricultural programs, and traditional efforts to promote conservation and resource protection.

My conscience rejects normalizing madness, so I will call the issues as I see them. If you disagree or find this objectionable—tough. Stop reading now and request a partial refund—you did make it halfway. Or you can look in a mirror and ask yourself what makes you so angry—your choice, while ours is still a democracy.

## RIDING THE TRAIN: THE BEST WAY TO SEE NATURE

Standing on the siding at Osceola, hearing the train whistle steaming in from the west, always brings me a thrill, knowing a journey is about to commence. Preparing for my April 2024 trip brought back many memories, especially about how much we used to travel when I was teaching and before Covid. It wasn't unusual for me to be away for 60 to 70 nights a year, with annual teaching stints in France and conferences, board meetings, and talks across the country. After many years as a 1K flyer on United, today we haven't been on a commercial jet in more than five years. Not traveling has allowed several things to happen. Perhaps most important the time to write books but also to engage more with our farm and garden, improving the design and doing projects like constructing a teahouse and a new greenhouse. It even led us to buy an additional 2 1/2 acres in front. Who knows, it may have saved us some money, though one of my travel rules was to use OPM—other people's money—whenever possible. I looked forward to this trip, to having the opportunity to visit Chicago, New York City, and Washington, D.C. The plan included old haunts familiar from my past, seeing friends like Amy and Chris, and connecting with people I hadn't seen for years like Gus Schumacher's widow, Susan. Travel is always a ripe source for planning future activities. Part of the "road to" idea involves my love for trains and Amtrak. I have been on most of its lines with the exception of the Texas Eagle, the far southern route, and some portions of the Coast Starlight north from San Francisco. Otherwise we have seen much of America by train, hoping for better trains but knowing we have to use the ones we have to ever see improvements.

What is it about train travel that makes it so evocative? As a boy on the farm with the windows open in the summer I could hear the whistle from the Prescott crossing four miles north. Perhaps it is nostalgia, the connection to pre-war times when everyone and everything moved by train—no interstate yet and air travel still in its infancy. There is the scenic dimension. Perhaps subconsciously this is the main draw: if you want to see the world through nature's lens you have to have a context for viewing nature. Flying from place to place is fast and convenient but only allows you to see places where you stop, not the vast areas between. Take the Zephyr, the Empire Builder, or the Southwest Chief across the western two thirds of the country and you gain a much different appreciation for the breath of the nation. You will come face to face with the enormity of our land, the miles of open prairie, grasslands, and deserts, the seemingly endless fields of farmland and pasture, and the rugged terrain of rocks and mountains and more across hundreds of miles. The same miles that early settlers and travelers had to cross, with little concept of the distances or obstacles facing them. To travel the Oregon Trail or to journey down the Santa Fe Trail was daunting and dangerous, yet these trails served tens of thousands seeking new opportunities, a fresh start, adventure, and freedom. Granted, going 80 miles an hour by train doesn't offer the same connection to nature as a wagon ride but it is a pace much more human than traveling by jetliner. Just the sense of the time involved breaks down any notion that this land is small. A three-hour plane ride might take two days and a night to cover by rail, but the vistas unfolding outside the window make every moment of the ride well worth the time.

## LOCAL ACTIONS CAN CAUSE BIG DAMAGES TO NATURE

As the last chapter proved, politics can affect nature in many ways. Typically large-scale actions are the threat, repealing a law, building a highway bridge, or constructing a power plant. Still, smaller political actions of a local nature can have significant effects on nature as well. The most common example is annexation of land, changing the jurisdiction from county to city. On its face, the decision may appear neutral for nature, but in reality such decisions can be significant, even a death sentence. We experienced this recently a few miles from our home. We often drive by a tree-covered hillside and valley along a creek, with large remnant oaks from a savanna. Some houses to the east and south and a new connector road had been built on the west side, but it was only when the bulldozers arrived that we witnessed a classic example of what the American Farmland Trust labeled decades ago the impermanence syndrome. Look around where you live, you can probably spot it too—land you know will sooner or later be converted to houses or other uses, away from the natural conditions it has enjoyed for centuries.

The key ingredients are these. It begins, officially, with annexation into a city with its goal to grow, add residents and increase the tax base. Next come the road improvements with accompanying infrastructure like sewer and water. Then all it needs are a willing seller and a developer ready to make their move. Once these are in place, the re-zoning plans are submitted to the community—the request is quickly scheduled for hearing and routinely approved—then the nature clock ticks down to zero. First come the clearing crews with bulldozers and chainsaws, who in a day can fell trees it took nature a century to grow. Next come the graders and dirt skinners to level, shape, and adjust the terrain to fit the plat and plan. They are followed by the concrete mixers to pave the streets and sidewalks. Now it has become building lots ready for homebuilders and buyers. They will "restore" nature by planting a few non-native shrubs and spindly saplings, hoping they will leaf out before they sell the home to move to a bigger and better one in another new subdivision.

Where do the owls nesting in the trees, the wood ducks living above the stream all go? How about the raccoons, possums, squirrels, and more who called the land home? We assume the animals must just move somewhere else. Good luck if you are a hatchling still in the nest or turtle eggs buried in the stream bank. Who knows and who cares what happens to these parts of nature! To be an afterthought you first have to be thought of, and none of our land use plans or procedures, the ones shaping how communities grow, gives much if any thought to nature. Sure the local conservation district and city development code may have rules to "control" soil erosion. Thus the straw-filled tubes you may see pinned around the edges of a project. These are our futile efforts to limit soil loss and protect water quality when it rains. Even these efforts are not primarily nature driven, instead they deal more with traffic safety from mud-slicked roads and complaints from nearby homes of silt-covered lawns.

Drainage ditches and their maintenance are another example of how official actions seemingly unrelated to nature can trigger major consequences. Iowa has thousands of miles of drainage ditches administered by hundreds of drainage districts, primarily in north central Iowa. Most districts and ditches have existed for over a century, their purpose being to drain the wetlands and create fertile farmland. The coming of the drainage ditch marked a disastrous decline for millions of acres of wetlands and the creatures residing there. Over time the ditches themselves became a substitute, poor as it may be, for nature. The grass and trees growing along the ditches may offer some of the few bits of remnant habitat and even become tree-lined corridors, serving as artificial streams in what otherwise are oceans of row crops. But therein lies the problem. To function, drainage ditches may need to be periodically maintained. You can read this to mean scraping them down to the ditch, removing the excess silt and piling it along the tops, cutting out all the trees, and destroying most of the habitat, all with little concern for whoever or whatever may call it home. It's important to remember that creating nature was never the purpose of drainage ditches—improving on nature was the goal!

In 2024 Frank Bruni published an outstanding book, *The Age of Grievance*, that captured much of what America is now seeing. As the title suggests, the book focuses on grievance and how it transforms and circulates through our nation's politics and culture. To begin, he notes grievance can be an important social force. It can be the precursor of justice and a prelude to enlightenment. In many ways the U.S. as a nation was born out of grievance. But it is important to recognize not all grievances are equal, and our inability to distinguish between what are essentially trivial, as captured so poignantly in the label "microaggressions," and what are significant, is one of our failings. In some ways discussions about grievance depend very much on who is speaking, because as Bruni notes what is at stake may be dueling definitions of freedom. This is certainly borne out in the now raging debate over the idea of DEI programs to promote diversity, equity, and inclusion. On the one hand, DEI can be seen as an important part of the nation's search for equality, while on the other hand the programs can be seen as repressive restraints on the freedom of individuals and businesses to make decisions. At this time the tide has certainly gone out on the DEI movement, as legislators in once welcoming states like Iowa race to ban and even outlaw teaching about or implementing DEI efforts. Whether DEI will ever "officially" return is uncertain, but its values can not be ignored.

The same dueling definitions of freedom are reflected in Iowa's new motto. Rather than being "a place to grow" or "fields of opportunity" we now have "freedom to flourish." It's unclear what the new freedoms are or what exactly will flourish. As you look across the state you might conclude the freedom being sought is to act without any responsibility to others.

Bruni does an excellent job of capturing what is driving grievance in America. Causes he points to are the ascendancy of social media, the breakdown of traditional media, increased income inequality, and a manner of individualism often indistinguishable from narcissism. As he notes, the U.S. has in many ways become an envy engine with increased focus on the evidence of inequality. In his view, many people have come to see America as being in a state of decline. It is certainly possible to see decline where we are now with nature in Iowa. We seem to have turned the ideas of hope and change from previous generations into tweak and tinker or, worse yet, worry and wither! One driver of conflict is our fixation on growth, on the idea we can always grow our way out of whatever crises we may face. Can we grow our way out of what we are doing to nature? What is wrong with a period of stability?

For America to work, we have to have optimism, and we have often found it in a program of growth. If growth presents its own challenges, this raises the question, What do we do instead to find optimism? The need for hope and how we can find it is the focus of chapter 8—what do we look forward to in the future? Bruni notes that one challenge relating to our expectations is the way we have an increasing belief in the sovereignty of the individual. This has deepened our tendency to weaken other forms of communal engagement and has turned people away from virtues like public spiritedness and perhaps even the idea of public property.

Bruni warns us that focusing only on grievance doesn't lead us to action but can strand us in inaction. We trade motion for commotion, and grievance can facilitate our retreat from responsibility, leaving us wallowing in being aggrieved. This danger is present in Iowa in our long debate over water quality. Breaking free from grievance to move toward action is what makes the formation of groups like the Driftless Water Defenders, discussed in chapter 9 about citizen justice, so important. As the election results of 2024 and its outcomes play out, it is possible that we will see the effect of Bruni's analysis. As he predicted, grievance coarsens our discussions and distances us from each other. Separation can nurture grievance, in contrast cooperation has traditionally been one of humanity's greatest strengths. We have the opportunity to use nature as an antidote to grievance, using it to promote cooperation, responsibility, and community progress, and to help us find a way forward. We need to be humble in how we use nature, because humility is itself an antidote to grievance.

## How Does Nature Feel about the 2024 Elections?

Well, the professor has made it clear that he is no fan of your new president. It is so like you humans to focus so much time and energy on short-term concerns. You very much live for the day, if not the hour. Understandable, I guess, since you have to face each day, get up, go to work, care for the kids, whatever it is that fills your time. Much of your experience may be shaped by politics and who is making the decisions shaping the economy and society.

As you realize, my experience is different, especially in my timing and horizon. The sun will shine, the rain will fall—or not—regardless of who wins the election. So the immediacy of the results, the joy or sorrow, is not something I experience, at least not directly. The effect of an election is felt more gradually in the larger decisions to come. Will you spend more money and effort to protect me, or will there be a loosening of safeguards, granting more rights and freedoms for you, if that is even possible? Will new rights be granted to the owners, the users, the abusers, the permit holders who request government permission to act, such as burying a pipeline, using it to sanctify and sanitize their actions? That is how the elections may effect me, but truthfully there may not be that much difference in what I experience, regardless of the outcomes. The processes, your procedures and attitudes, for dealing with me, at least officially, are relatively stable. This is in keeping with your idea of being a nation of laws, if that truth is still valid, as I hope it is.

I may experience the impact of the elections results in a way that is more indirect but no less real—in how the results influence the actions of the people in direct contact with nature. For the sake of simplicity, I think of people being in two general categories, recognizing the imperfections of such binary characterizations. On the one hand, there are the nature protectors, the nature lovers, the advocates who want the best for me, as they see it. The other group I call the users, or more accurately, the consumers of nature, recognizing that even the advocates for protecting nature—me—just see my use in a different way. The second group is different. They see me as something to be harnessed and put to work, primarily to yield economic gains or experiences. If this can be done privately and exclusively, then even better.

It is interesting to see how these two groups experience elections. The second group may carry on as if there's no real effect. This is true because, for the most part, under your laws, they were already in control of nature. Their relative freedom to act is often the status quo. If there is a change, they may feel even more emboldened, secure in the knowledge no one is going to tell them no or place new restraints on their actions. As to our first group, my protectors, the effect of the 2024 elections, widely seen as a dark, even tragic day for so-called progressive issues (for better or worse this is where most people place nature), is mixed. They are deeply disheartened, concerned the political winds bode ill for me or at least for their favorite nature cause, as the professor has explained.

Ironically, the tragic outcome may spur them to greater efforts, even leading to a search for more creative approaches. This is true for several reasons. The political results may mean more traditional routes of nature work will be closed off, like new legal protections, legislation, or more public funding. This doesn't mean they will give up. Instead, they will shift the focus to other efforts, for example, encouraging landowners to protect their land and private fundraising to complete major projects. Granted this takes more work and is more individualized, but it can be liberating, free from government restraints or requirements. They may have to work harder, but this may help clarify their purpose, forcing them to focus on identifying the individuals, projects, and institutions that want to help. No doubt, the availability of public funding or incentives is valuable. But it can also lull you into doing things the government way, as with various USDA conservation programs. The programs are valuable but have their own costs and limitations. You earn your money, assuming the USDA will still honor the legal contracts you signed!

A second reason for a renewed focus on private efforts is understandable, perhaps even predictable. Faith in making progress via the political route is always tempered by the traditional challenges, such as resistance from the Farm Bureau. Even in good times, hoped for progress may prove illusory. Vivid proof is the sad failure of Iowa lawmakers to raise the sales tax to support the Natural Resources Trust fund, 15 years since its addition to the Constitution. These years of inaction follow the nearly 10 years supporters spent bringing the trust fund to the ballot for Iowa voters. Consider the time, energy, and money expended in this more than two decades of effort, still without a penny in the fund! Failure to fund the trust is the watched kettle that never boils. Now the forces long opposed to funding the trust argue this failure is reason to jettison the idea. They have become emboldened enough to introduce legislation to replace it with a slush fund for property tax relief! This fight is one I hope Iowans eventually win, but there are lessons to be learned from other efforts. Consider the more productive outcomes—and the overwhelming public support shown for recent nature bonding campaigns in Polk, Johnson, and Story Counties, authorizing over $100 million in nature funding. It may be that local efforts for specific projects have more success than general and ambitious—but vague—state funding efforts.

## NATURE AND POLITICS: THINKING ABOUT THE ISSUES

As nature explains, it takes the long look when it comes to politics and doesn't fear the outcome of elections. This is a luxury we don't have, in part because our lives are shorter and the impact of political decisions is something we feel more immediately. From a human perspective this reality makes politics and voting a central issue, regarding both the future of nature, what is done to it and what parts remain, as well as how we experience the natural world. Look at the critical issues facing us in Iowa—the $CO_2$ pipeline, the lack of enforcement for polluting the Nishnabotna River, and the liberal granting of water withdrawal permits. Clearly most of these matters will be resolved in a political world.

The politics of those elected or appointed to decide are influenced by their personal ideologies. Politics are also influenced by the desires of supporters, voters, and their funders. You see this from the Iowa Senator who during the 2024 legislative session was able to prevent any consideration of the legislation to rein in using eminent domain for $CO_2$ pipelines, a nice favor for his friends at Summit Carbon Solutions. But he wasn't able to repeat the favor in 2025 when his Senate colleagues forced a vote on the legislation, that is until the Governor's veto of the bill led to the same outcome. A related goal is to avoid angering supporters or incurring their wrath. This explains why most members of the Iowa General Assembly, on both sides of the aisle, are hesitant to raise the idea agriculture and water pollution have connections to the Iowa cancer story. Doing so would bring the weight of the Iowa agricultural community down upon them.

One result of these influences is inaction. Another result is searching for other issues, distractions to make it appear work is being done. You see this in how the legislature avoids increasing state funding for acquiring new public lands, as voters supported in 2010 when creating the natural resources trust fund, and now reflected in county nature bonds. Instead of new funding, opponents turn to claiming the state can't take care of the land it has so why acquire more? This ruse is especially galling since any budget shortfalls to maintain state parks result from the Legislature underfunding DNR. The underfunding is in part designed to create the problem and provide the excuse for not doing more. Deferred maintenance on park facilities, unmown fields, and shortage of park staff do not indicate the public doesn't want more nature; instead they reveal legislators aren't providing needed funding.

Politics play out at all levels, from state and local to national. County supervisors set funding for the county conservation system and appoint the five commissioners. The outstanding work of this part of the Iowa nature community is described in chapter 7. The counties are bright spots, but their variations can be stark. In some counties, even ones like Winneshiek with a tourism-dependent economy, the opponents of nature are willing to oppose additional nature funding. Their failure to appreciate the significant contributions nature and outdoor recreation provide the local economy is telling. At the state level, the politicization of nature is readily apparent, but even with opposition there are reasons for hope, ideas explored in chapter 8.

At the national level, the results of the last three presidential elections led to pendulum-like shifts in policy and priorities for nature. When the first Trump administration followed eight years of Obama, a campaign to reverse environmental gains was clearly implemented. Most symbolically it was marked by efforts to reduce the size of recently created national monuments, notably Bears Ears and Grand Staircase Escalante in Utah. Elsewhere, the radical decision to move the national headquarters of the Bureau of Land Management from D.C. to Grand Junction, Colorado, was meant to curry favor with those who use and exploit federal public lands in the West. These actions were facilitated by the appointment of government officials with stark antina-ture agendas, including the Secretary of the Interior and others. When the Biden administration came to power, the pattern was repeated but in reverse. National monuments were restored, government rules on exploiting federal lands, particularly for energy production and min-ing, were reversed, and new leaders were put in place. Most notable was the appointment of Deb Haaland, the first Native American to hold a cabinet position, to run the Department of the Interior. Her selection was especially poignant given the legacy of neglect and mal-administration Interior has inflicted on the nation's tribes. After the Biden-Harris reset, new actions were taken, like expanding nation-al monuments and creating new ones—and the proposed Bureau of Land Management rule providing for conservation leases on public lands—issues discussed in chapter 7.

Unfortunately but predictably, restoration of the Trump administra-tion reversed the pendulum, and we are now in the midst of rejecting most Biden actions, with an even harder and more exploitive attitude toward nature. Reversing any actions referring to climate change and heightening the push for domestic energy production through fossil fuels to the exclusion of cleaner alternatives like wind and solar mean nature will bear the brunt of many new efforts. As we think about the pendulum swings of national policy relating to nature, we can perhaps better appreciate the wisdom in nature's perspective on elections. It will continue and thrive, in its own ways, regardless of the actions we take in the short time we are here to make them.

As disturbing and even traumatic as the new administration's policies are for nature, they should not come as a surprise if you were paying attention. Even though tragic, they do provide a good opportunity to identify possible lessons to draw and ideas to consider for moving forward.

First is to recognize policies and law can change. While laws may be difficult to enact, they can be changed. They are not permanent. Even tattoos can be removed! Granted the changes usually take many years. Consider the long-term plan of Republicans and the business community to reduce the power of administrative agencies. This 30-year effort came to a head in 2023 when the U.S. Supreme Court reversed what is known as the *Chevron* doctrine, the idea the courts should defer to agency interpretations of their rules implementing legislative intent. The *Chevron* doctrine, in place for 50 years, was an important precedent for allocating the relative power between administrative agencies and federal courts. The doctrine supported the expertise of agencies and protected courts from needing to engage in detailed considerations of every challenged action. It allowed the courts to reserve their attention for issues where the stakes were greater or support for the agency interpretation was lacking. With *Chevron* reversed, many important legal precedents, such as rules applying to the Clean Water Act, are now in doubt and new lines of attack have opened for any agency rule making.

A second lesson is changes from shifts in national policy relating to nature shouldn't come as a surprise because resistance or opposition to the law and policies is no secret. It's important to recognize opposition to any law or policy is almost essentially a given. Laws are typically enacted to either restrain some behavior or to impose a tax on activities. As a result, opposition is known and telegraphed, making it apparent and predictable. Even so, stealth can certainly come into play when drastic changes are considered.

It's dangerous for those who believe they are in control of the agenda to assume they will always remain in control. It is also dangerous to assume once enacted, laws and policies will become so ingrained in our culture and economy that no one will dare to challenge them. The political debate and legal reversals on reproductive freedom illustrate the dangers of such misguided assumptions. Believing your policies are so popular they can survive any change in political regimes means such hubris can catch you with your nature pants down.

For the most part, even though nature issues are important and enjoy widespread support within the nature crowd, it is important to recognize most citizens do not consider nature a critical issue on the national political agenda. Other concerns like inflation, employment, imports, and the border take center stage. As a result, nature issues don't receive a great deal of political attention or necessarily garner strong voter support. This make it easier for politicians to ignore them or claim that nature must yield to higher priorities.

Politically and financially, the lesson for nature projects is the need to diversify financial and political support if possible with private funding and support from foundations and their members. These sources can be more secure and can offer more flexibility as to their use. The funding may not be as large as obtaining a federal grant, but there will certainly be fewer strings attached. In recent years organizations like Practical Farmers of Iowa were awarded large USDA grants under the regional conservation partnership program or RCPP. It can take organizations months and years to deal with administrative hurdles to get contracts approved by the USDA. The Iowa Natural Heritage Foundation was the recipient of a large federal grant in 2023 to help create and restore 10,000 acres of protected grasslands in Iowa. It is not clear when or if the project will ever begin. With the change in administrations the worry is projects like this will be canceled by the USDA, or worse yet terminated once work has begun.

The financial risk from relying on federal funding is especially real if funds are used to employ staff or launch new programs. This makes it a priority to only hire staff with so-called hard money rather than relying on soft money through grants. Reducing dependence on government or political sources can lead to several alternatives. One way of diversifying fundraising, while serving the needs of members and the nature community, is increasing efforts at planned giving. The loyalty and support members have for an organization's mission, combined with confidence in the long-term stability and quality of its leadership, can lead to conversations about what comes next for them and their land. As the land knows, we all want to live forever but won't. On the other hand, the land will remain. Who will be its steward? It may be possible to focus on individual support to obtain land, if long-term members are aging and own significant tracts of nature-rich land they want to protect. Another alternative? Looking for creative ways to generate income using entrepreneurial efforts to harness staff capacity to offer land management or use land resources for activities like prairie seed harvesting.

Here's another important political lesson from the recent election, nature's advocates need to appreciate how strongly the opponents fear or resist nature protections. They see the policies as restraints on economic opportunities, whether to mine, drill, farm, drain, log, or whatever exploitive activity may be desired. As a result, nature's advocates can't imagine how quick or punitive the pushback may be—they can't believe someone actually wants to cut down those trees or drill in a pristine valley. Failure of imagination can lead to underestimating the wrath of those opposed to elevating nature protection over economics.

One final lesson: It will require vigilance and more concerted organizing and political work by nature's advocates to become effective, to make gains, and to defend them. Organizations will need to lean into the energy and passion of young people, an important but still widely untapped political force. Youth will play a critical role in future years, particularly on issues like climate, something they see affecting their future opportunities. While our concerns for climate may be momentarily set back, they aren't going away. The importance of organizing members and voters around the value of nature helps identify another ingredient missing in the politics of Iowa's nature dynamic.

## VOTE FOR NATURE: A NEW COALITION FOR IOWA'S NATURE COMMUNITY

In *World In Their Hands: Original Thinkers, Doers, Fighters and the Future of Conservation*, Steve Johnson reviews the contributions of many nature leaders, dividing them into thinkers, doers, and fighters. One person discussed is David Brower, most famous for his work with the Sierra Club and, after leaving it, for founding the Friends of the Earth. The book notes he also helped found its sister organization, the League of Conservation Voters. Mention of the league led me to wonder why have I never heard of the Iowa League of Conservation Voters. The answer is easy—there isn't one! There are over 30 state affiliates, but the map shows a large swath of the Midwest not covered, including Iowa. There must be a story why Iowans never seized this opportunity, but this begs a better question, What will it take to create something like an Iowa League of Conservation Voters? Thinking about it, I realized this may be a key ingredient missing in the Iowa nature story—a political arm for the environment, conservation, and nature community.

Clearly we have many outstanding nature-focused organizations, but we do not have one devoted solely to the politics of getting people out to vote for nature. Because we do not have a political group focused on nature, we lack the ability to provide a coordinated response to political campaigns waged by the Iowa Farm Bureau and others against nature. The opposition to expanding public lands and using regulations to address chronic failures of voluntary efforts are just two examples of political issues in need of resistance. Thinking about creating an Iowa Nature Voters organization is an opportunity to consider what it might provide and why creating it may prove beneficial. Here are some ideas for what it might offer.

Focus - The main feature would be the focus on politics, voting, and legislative action. Many conservation and nature groups in Iowa such as the Iowa Natural Heritage Foundation, the Ike's, and the Iowa Environmental Council employee lobbyists, but their focus is typically narrow and somewhat parochial, and the organizations' ability to engage in active political work is hindered by their nonprofit status.

Comprehensive - No one organization can do it all, and each needs to set its priorities, but the Iowa Nature Voters could have a broader base of issues or, as the British would say its remit. Its agenda could include public lands, water quality, and funding for parks, trails, and wildlife areas such as in the Resource Enhancement and Protection or REAP program. Its work could include all these and more, like addressing how Iowa grants water use permits and enforces environmental laws.

Coalition building - There are examples of coalitions in the Iowa nature community—the Iowa Environmental Council is one—and the coalition formed to support funding the Natural Resources Trust is another. However, these coalitions typically focus on one issue or are identified with one organization. This can limit their reach; for example, the Iowa Environmental Council is not widely appreciated by many sportsmen's groups, who see it as opposed to their nature-based activities like hunting and trapping. A political organization devoted solely to building a coalition among nature voters could work to avoid partisan and parochial divides with a simple message: Vote for Nature.

Common ground - Rather than illuminating what might divide conservation and environmental groups along interest lines, the Iowa Nature Voters could serve to elevate and highlight their shared values and priorities, including:

respect for nature,

the need to increase protection and enhancement of nature,

the desire to increase opportunities for the public to engage with nature,

the promotion of nature-based education in schools,

the reasonable use of regulations to set standards of land and water stewardship,

the predictable and responsible administration of laws and the performance of duties by government actors, and

the power to speak in nature's voice in political debates, to promote justice and respect.

Even if there are benefits from creating an Iowa Nature Voters organization, there are arguments for why it is not needed. These may come from those now working in the area who are threatened by a new organization. Predictable reactions and questions may include:

Will it duplicate current efforts?

Will it compete for funding, for media attention, and for politicians' time?

Will it confuse voters about the issues if the message differs from other voices?

Whom does it represent, and what is its source of power?

Where such an organization draws its political power from opens several possibilities. It could be the number of members represented who provide the political heft to get attention from politicians. Look across the sweep of Iowa nature-related organizations. It is clear tens of thousands of Iowans are involved in nature pursuits, from prairie enthusiasts and bird watchers, from hunters and anglers, to boaters and hikers. The various associations created to protect the Iowa Great Lakes in northwest Iowa have thousands of members, the Izaak Walton League of Iowa over 10,000, and Iowa Natural Heritage Foundation at least 12,000. Audubon has thousands more. The power could also be in the money raised to use as political contributions. A key source of power could be the knowledge represented and the clarity of the message, especially if the organization is trusted and respected for knowing its business.

There are other questions to address in creating any political organization of this type. How would it be funded, who would do the work, how would its actions and priorities be determined, and how would decisions be made and by whom? These questions need to be addressed in any organizational initiative. More importantly, is creating an organization to represent Iowa's nature voters a Big Idea we need to consider? It could be the missing ingredient to address what is now limiting the ability of nature and environmental nonprofits to compete more aggressively in the political arena. It could be an important vehicle to aid in the search for hope in Iowa's nature future.

# Chapter 7
# Land Is Nature's Face: Private Property and Public Need

I began writing *The Land Remains* four years ago, focusing on the role land played in my family and in our society. Exploring the future of nature is possible only by acknowledging the role of land and legal questions of its ownership. American property laws have evolved over generations and are now well settled, offering confidence to buyers, sellers, and owners of land that their rights are secure. This does not mean landownership is no longer a topic of active political discussion and even possible change and reform. The link between land ownership and the health and fate of nature is inseparable. Even the most casual observer can see how the existence and future of what we consider nature—what exists on top of the land—are shaped by the desires of who owns the land.

In our society, the relationship is controlled by laws in the form of property rights. If there are disputes, such as about using eminent domain, our justice system decides who has the right to own and determine how the land is used. All the focus on land and the power it offers is directed at the interests and identities of the individuals who own it. The interests or needs of nature are not really part of the discussion and instead are secondary, if that. The assumption appears to be that nature will be enhanced when landownership is held by those with more nature beneficent-attitudes, the Leopoldians. Some suggest indigenous people have this as well, assuming they hold more benign and balanced views toward nature and land. Even here the interests of nature are still distilled only through the attitudes of the owners, even if the players and playing pieces are shuffled and redealt. We will probably never see a time when the interests of nature are the paramount consideration in shaping its future. Even so, the history of our nation and the evolution of our laws relating to nature can and do reflect a respect for the land, revealing it as the face of nature.

## Who Are My Friends?

My friends come in all shapes and sizes, from school kids visiting a prairie, to lawmakers wielding a pen, to local conservation officials maintaining a park, to local residents eager for exercise outdoors to bird watch, fish, hunt, bike, or however they enjoy being with me. All these friends play important roles in supporting me, helping safeguard my future, and reminding you of the vital role I play in your lives. One group of my friends deserves special attention, not necessarily because they are more worthy—you are all equal in my eyes—but because of how they have used the opportunities their families have been given to protect and add to my future.

These are the landowners, the stewards, who decide to permanently protect their land so its natural traits, whatever they might be, can continue in the future. These are the families like the Garsts, who created the Whiterock Conservancy, a 5,000 acre land trust consisting of oak savanna, prairies, and river lands near Coon Rapids. They are people like Jan and Tom Lovell. They donated over 2,000 feet of shoreline and hundreds of acres along Clear Lake, creating with a neighbor the largest undeveloped shoreline park on this important glacial lake. It is a family like the DeCooks in Monroe County. They assembled and protected more than 3,000 acres of rolling hillsides and valleys, restoring them, they would say rewilding, to my presettlement state.

The actions of these friends can take many forms such as donating land to a land trust like the Iowa Natural Heritage Foundation or creating permanent conservation easements so even though the land is still privately owned its natural values are safeguarded. This is the story of the 800 acres of Twin Valleys, north of Decorah owned by the Seed Savers Exchange and protected under an easement to the USDA and the INHF. The permanent protection of land can come through sale or donation to a county conservation board or to the federal government or state for use as public land. The point is if landowners want to see their land and my nature permanently protected, there are many ways to do so.

The history and role of individuals and families using their land and treasure to protect nature are long and rich. One woman, known to all of you who have read her children's books, helped lead the early history of land protection in the United Kingdom. Beatrix Potter, known to millions as the creator of Peter Rabbit, Jemima Puddle-Duck, Mr. Jeremy Fisher and other beloved creatures, spent her life conserving land in England's Lake District. In life as Mrs. Hellis, a breeder and protector of her beloved Herdwick sheep, she protected several thousand acres of Fell lands, eventually donating them to the public. Her story is inspiring and hopeful, a preview of the work of families like those mentioned. You may not be in a position to donate or protect land for me and the public, but if you are, I encourage you to consider doing so. The donation the Professor and Khanh made over 20 years ago to create Hamilton Prairie for the Adams County Conservation Board remains one of the most meaningful acts they will take in their lifetimes.

## LAND AS THE FACE OF NATURE

As we think about the span of environmental and nature concerns and the range of issues involved, from wildlife and wilderness, to water quality and wellness, to weather and climate change, there is one common denominator: they are all linked to the land—how it is used, what grows there, who owns it. In so many ways land is what we see when we open our eyes, making land the face of nature. It is the canvas where we paint our lives, it is the foundation under the cultures we build, and it is the home where nature exists. All of our lives are linked to it—the water, the air, the living world—are all linked in their own way to the land.

As nature's face, the land provides our most effective tool for looking through nature's lens. The history of our relation to nature is largely reflected in how we have chosen to use the land. In the first book in this trilogy, *The Land Remains*, I explored the many issues highlighting our history with the land, from its acquisition and distribution to its harnessing and exploitation. All the episodes are replete with people, policies, and actions whose ramifications continue to echo today. The stories and the people shaping our relations to the land are manifold, from Jefferson to Lacey, from Muir to Darling, from Leopold to Bromfield, and from the Roosevelts to Wallace, plus many more. Our history on the land has been told by brilliant scholars like Andro Linklater and Jedediah Purdy, whose insights have shaped my writing. Douglas Brinkley's biographies of the Roosevelts and Rachel Carson and the Silent Spring Revolution all enrich the story.

An important book from 1981 fleshes out the history of our relations to land. In *The American Conservation Movement: John Muir and His Legacy*, Stephen Fox uses Muir as the fountainhead and traces the evolution of the conservation movement as shaped by the organizations, individuals, and policies they promoted. The growing role for public lands, from timber reserves to national parks—and the conflicts over how best to use these lands—pitted the growing influence of Gifford Pinchot's wise use philosophy, (which mostly means cutting our forests), against the preservation ethic personified by Muir and the legions he influenced. In the first half of the 20th century, the creation and growth of conservation groups marked America's emerging conservation concerns. The wildlife efforts by hunters and sportsmen led to important developments like the creation in 1922 of the Izaak Walton League. Another important step was the emergence of the Audubon Society into a national effort. Years later, wilderness protection was added to the nature choir, a natural outgrowth from the early efforts of Muir, as manifested by the Sierra Club he helped found as a mountaineering social club.

Fox explains how this movement centered on several major themes. The first set the terms for the evolution of our philosophy in relation to nature, experienced as a broadening of perspective from the traditional view nature exists only to serve man, the philosophy of U.S. land distribution policy, to Muir's philosophy recognizing humans as just one component of nature. This community of nature philosophy eloquently stated by Aldo Leopold in his "land ethic" essay premised a right for nature to exist not just as commodified for human use but as its own entity. This broader view of nature challenged the notion, as one commentator put it, "man is the one big toad in the puddle of life."

Fox identifies many early conservation leaders as "radical amateurs," rather than people whose livelihoods depended on using nature or working for those who did. These leaders of the evolving web of conservation efforts were drawn to the work by their love and passion for nature. Many had childhood experiences sharing time with nature, bird watching being a common pursuit. Their existence as radical amateurs fueled their willingness to challenge society's conventional thinking and to confront entrenched economic powers, like the lumber barons or the gun manufacturers. But the amateur status held weaknesses, a lack of organization and often a shortage of funds, unless the advocates came from independent means.

These nature leaders were primarily drawn from the middle class and with few exceptions were male and white, giving the movement a less than democratized history. There are amazing figures from this period, whose stories need to be told. One is Will Dilg, who helped found the Izaak Walton League in 1922. His greatest accomplishment was leading the Ikes in supporting the 1924 initiative for Congress to authorize spending $1.5 million to acquire the 300,000 acres creating the Upper Mississippi River Wildlife and Fish Refuge. This gem of nature we now take for granted, was slated to be drained to create more farmland. Only through the work of Dilg, the Izaak Walton League, and the 2 million members of the General Federation of Women's Clubs, were they able to turn the tide.

The wetlands, islands, and web of river channels protected by the new refuge extend over 150 miles from Dubuque, IA, to Winona, MN, making it an invaluable part of the migratory flyway and a fish hatchery for the river. The story of Will Dilg has largely fallen from memory but one man, Steve Marking, who calls himself a Riverlorian is changing that. Marking wrote and performs a fascinating one-man show concerning Dilg, the Ikes, and creation of the Upper Mississippi Fish and Wildlife Refuge, which just celebrated its 100th Anniversary.

A second notable leader from this era is Rosalie Edge, who thorough her one person Emergency Conservation Committee became perhaps the most influential conservation policy voice bridging the 1920s to postwar era. Her tireless efforts and sharp elbows made Edge the first American woman to achieve renown as a national conservation leader. She brought unwanted attention to the early history of the Audubon Society colluding with the gun lobby for funding by allowing trapping on its reserves. Her years of scolding led to reforms helping Audubon gain the prestige it has today. Most importantly she is known for her personal efforts to save Hawk Mountain the raptor overlook in Eastern Pennsylvania. It exists today because Edge stepped in to purchase the mountain top with her own funds. She hired the employees who guarded access to the pass where locals slaughtered thousands of hawks and raptors riding low on the wind currents. Her life story is told in rich detail by Dyan Zaslowsky in *Rosalie Edge, Hawk of Mercy: The Activist Who Saved Nature from the Conservationists.*

Over time the conservation groups founded by people like Dilg and Edge needed to hire professional staff to manage the growing organizations. This transition set up an organizational tension you can see today in many nonprofits between the professional staff, whose jobs depend on stability and funding, and boards of directors, who may be more willing to challenge the status quo and not shirk from controversy, even when it might threaten funders, sponsors, and friends.

Another insight from Fox concerns the evolution of the conservation movement to today's environmental movement. The shift from conservation to ecology and then to the environment reflected a shift from the more utilitarian ideas inherent in conservation, such as more efficient resource use, to the more preservationist or restorative aspects of a broader environmental perspective. This perspective may even question the wisdom of the use in the first place. Most of us grew up in the era of environmentalism, meaning we have not contemplated the effect of the evolution from conservation to the environment.

I found one of Fox's observations challenging to accept. In his view the main goal and effect of the shift to environmentalism were to turn our focus away from nature and back to humans. The concerns of the 1970s were how nuclear fallout would harm our health, how pesticides might affect food safety, and whether the population bomb would bring privation. This reorientation of the focus to humans away from nature changed the debate, perhaps broadening the audience to include those who now feared the outcomes but weakening attention to nature or how its components might fare.

I found this view challenging in part because in over 40 years of working on environmental matters I have never considered the main objective to be people and not nature. My conclusion is Fox's observation is in part a function of the time he was writing and his own misgivings for the ways traditional conservation concerns were being supplanted by the new environmental awareness. If you consider the history of what has happened since Fox wrote, the focus of many environmental groups has, at least in my perspective, returned to nature. Consider the work of the Sierra Club across a broad range of environmental concerns, or the World Wildlife Fund, or the National Wildlife Federation, or the outstanding publications from the National Audubon Society. When was the last time you read an article raising or even referencing the specter of the population bomb or nuclear wastes? It is almost surprising, even frightening really, how little we consider population, especially given our growing concerns about climate.

Fox was writing in 1981, meaning he was too early to observe the rapid growth of a critically important sector of the nature community: the land trust movement. Today groups like The Nature Conservancy, the Trust for Public Land, the American Farmland Trust and others have collectively protected over 60 million acres of land in the United States. This is more land than in all of the national parks. These privately funded and operated not-for-profit land trusts are playing a critical role in building on public land protections and offering private owners ways to conserve their land. The Land Trust Alliance, the national umbrella group representing land trusts, has over 1,100 members from across the nation. One charter member is the Iowa Natural Heritage Foundation, about which I have written often with more to come in chapter 8. I'm proud the INHF, now in its 45th year, recently protected its 200,000th acre of Iowa land. Land trusts help illuminate the premise of this chapter: land is the face of nature. The breadth of land trusts means few parts of the natural world are outside their focus.

Thinking about the issue of public lands raises many important political questions. At the federal level, there are the ongoing conflicts over the future of public lands in the western states. There is no legal question that the federal government both owns these lands and is under no obligation to either privatize or to pass them to the states, but the politics of the matter are a different question. Many western states are home to millions of acres of federal land not within national parks or national forests or otherwise designated for specific federal uses. These lands are largely controlled by the Bureau of Land Management, and most are subject to private use through grazing contracts, mineral leases, and other agreements. Since the 1880s when the federal government began slowing distribution of land from the federal domain, political pressure in western states has clamored for more. More in the sense of more lands made available for private ownership and more in the sense of local control for the states, with the counterpart being fewer lands owned or controlled by the federal government.

Today the future of federal lands in the West is still very much in play. It is seen in the actions of state politicians like those in Montana and Utah who demand that federal lands be returned to the states to be sold for private uses. It is reflected in litigation challenging the Bureau of Land Management decision to consider conservation as a legitimate public use suitable for competitive bidding on lands, now largely dedicated to consumptive uses like grazing. Unfortunately, the outcome of the 2024 elections will significantly affect how these issues fare. You need look no farther for proof of this than the effort by some Senate Republicans to add a provision to the recently enacted "big, beautiful tax bill" requiring the federal government to sell up to 3.3 million acres of public lands, a proposal that set off a predictable firestorm of opposition. The good news is - for now - the idea was rejected, but no doubt efforts to privatize part of the public lands we all own as citizens will continue.

The question of public lands policy, while primarily a federal issue, is not off limits for the states. In recent years the question of whether Iowa should acquire more land for public use has become a politicized mess, largely at the behest of the Iowa Farm Bureau and its affiliated politicians. This may seem surprising given Iowa's rank of 49th in the nation in percentage of land in public ownership. But this has not limited its political potency. Every year Republican legislators attempt to enact some new proposed law to restrict how and if the state can acquire more land for parks, trails, and wildlife areas. Some observers even believe the politics of acquiring more public lands is the main reason the Iowa legislature has failed for 15 years to pass a sales tax increase to fund the natural resources trust fund.

## JOHN LACEY: ONE OF NATURE'S BEST FRIENDS STILL DELIVERING AFTER 120 YEARS

One of the nation's most important but unheralded friends of nature was John F. Lacey from Oskaloosa, Iowa. If you read *The Land Remains,* you may remember the story of Congressman Lacey and his contributions to U.S. conservation policy at the turn of the last century.

In case you haven't, here is the short version. It involves history, federal land policy, protecting nature, fierce opposition from the representatives of the exploiters, namely, timber, energy, and mining companies, and the role of legislation. Most importantly for us, the story of Lacey's legacy continues to resonate today. He was elected to Congress in the 1890s after serving for many years as a railroad lawyer in Oskaloosa. He served in Congress for 16 years. From his position as chair of the House Committee on Public Lands he wielded broad influence as a champion for wildlife and public lands. Most notably, birders may know him from the Lacey Act, which protects birds from commercial exploitation, a law now expanded to cover trees and other plant materials. Lacey's promotion of the wise use of resources, including retaining land under federal control, placed him in the vanguard of the emerging conservation movement. His legislation established the framework for what became the national forest system, and another of his laws did the same for setting the guidelines for national parks.

Lacey's most significant contribution to federal policy on nature, the law most relevant today, was the 1906 Antiquities Act. The law gives the president unilateral power to designate lands in the federal domain with scenic, historic, and scientific value as national monuments, protected from some forms of commercial consumptive exploitation. Lacey's opponents in Congress didn't appreciate the breadth of the legislation, believing its use constrained to small areas. They soon discovered their error, as the law contains no such limitation. Over the next 18 months, President Theodore Roosevelt, who referred to his friend Congressman Lacey as "the man" when it came to conservation, used the Antiquities Act eighteen times to protect thousands of acres of unique scenic and historic areas. Many are familiar to us today: Devils Tower, Mesa Verde, the Petrified Forest, and even the Grand Canyon.

The sweep and potential of the Antiquities Act may have been beyond even Lacey's imagination. Since its enactment 18 presidents have used the law, only Presidents Nixon, Reagan, and Bush the First did not. Today the nation has 136 national monuments protecting hundreds of millions of acres of land. The Antiquities Act was in the news in early January 2025, when in one of his last official acts President Biden created two new national monuments in California. The Chuckwalla National Monument covers over 624,000 acres, and the Sattitla Highlands National Monument protects another 224,000 acres. Together with earlier forms of federal protection, these new national monuments help create a 600-mile swath of protected lands stretching from southern California to Moab. During his time in office President Biden created 10 new national monuments, expanded two already in existence, and restored three that his predecessor had attempted to significantly reduce in size. His actions were part of his larger America the Beautiful initiative, with the goal of the federal government protecting 30% of the nation's land and waters.

Of course no good deed by the Biden administration will go untarnished by the vindictive reach of the new administration. Predictably, in early March 2025 the Department of the Interior announced, at least temporarily before the press release was withdrawn, that the two new California national monuments were being withdrawn. This is par for the course. The current occupant of the White House attempted the same thing for Bears Ears and Grand Staircase Escalante. The litigation challenging the attempt to reduce their size became moot when Biden restored them. Now the nation may finally get an answer from the courts about whether a president can reverse a predecessor's creation of a national monument. In late May 2025 the Office of the Legal Counsel published a 50 page memorandum written by Lanora Pettit, Deputy Assistance Attorney General, titled "Revocation of Prior Monument Designations" ruling the President has the Authority to modify previously established National Monuments by concluding they never were or are no longer deserving of Antiquity Act protections. Whether the federal courts will accept this new and revised legal analysis is to be seen.

As this drama indicates, creating national monuments, like any effort to protect federal land from further exploitation, is not without controversy. This is certainly the case for the proposed federal rule issued by the Bureau of Land Management in summer 2024 to expand approved purposes for leasing federal land to include mitigation and restoration, commonly referred to as conservation leasing. The rule is being challenged by the predictable western forces representing the grazing sector, forestry, energy exploration, and mining, as well as by state and local officials and hopeful privatizers, all gathered under the amorphous banner of "state's rights." All believe the BLM cannot authorize such conservation "uses." Their main argument is that conservation or mitigation is not really a use justified under the applicable federal law. Their theory is because the leases will not involve some type of active extractive or consumptive use of the lands, they are not uses at all. In a nutshell, to them nature is of human value only when it is being consumed or harnessed for production. This presumption captures our historic attitude toward federal lands and nature. The effort of the Biden administration and the BLM to expand our view of how nature can be used to include the concept of conservation is revolutionary. It also makes common sense—promoting both multiple and wise uses, all in the public interest. Remember that the land is owned by the public. Lacey would no doubt approve of the BLM's proposal.

Unfortunately you could expect it was only a matter of time until the new Secretary of the Interior withdrew the proposed BLM rule as being too woke, even tarring it with the dreaded DEI label. New Secretary of the Interior Doug Burgum has his marching orders: unleash America's fossil fuels. If this means opening up wildlife reserves for drilling or repealing other environmental protections—tough! In March 2025, the Iowa Naturalists invited me to speak at their annual meeting, and because it was in Oskaloosa, my topic was the history of John Lacey and what he did to establish the nation's protections for nature. His words are just as relevant today if not more relevant. "The immensity of man's power to destroy imposes a responsibility to preserve."

The news in the days before my talk were filled with stories of hundreds of federal employees—with the National Park Service, the USDA, the U.S. Fish and Wildlife Service, and other agencies—being summarily fired from their jobs for no reason other than to satisfy the ego of a megalomaniac billionaire unleashed on the federal government. Many of these people are naturalists, like the audience I was addressing. As a result, I could not ignore the opportunity to share what I believe Congressman Lacey—himself a conservative Republican—would say about what is happening in our nation. Lacey would have these three reactions:

He would be outraged at the impact on nature and the firing of the professionals trained and hired to protect it.

He would be appalled by the overreach and arrogance of the president and the executive branch in usurping unbridled Kinglike powers to defy the rules of law and Congressional intent.

He would be disgusted by the willingness of members of Congress, including all the Iowa delegation, to abandon their oversight duty and powers to the President.

I was startled when after making these remarks, the audience burst into applause. Nature does have friends.

## Iowa's Secret Sauce for Protecting Nature: the County Conservation System

The radical shift in federal attitudes toward protecting nature and public lands makes it important to consider opportunities for state action. Although many of the same political forces opposing nature can be found here, we have more power to enhance efforts to protect nature. Many Iowans don't appreciate how, even with our intensive agriculture, our state has managed to create a broad array of local parks, wildlife areas, and other natural facilities available for public use, over 2,000 at last count. The secret is Iowa's unique system of county conservation commissions, which form a broad network of nature facilities and programming. The idea to authorize a local park system was first proposed in 1943, but it wasn't until 1955 that the Iowa General Assembly enacted the law creating the county conservation system. By the next year, 16 counties had commissions, and by the 1980's, all 99 counties had one. The idea is simple and straightforward. The County Board of Supervisors creates the commission and appoints five citizens on the conservation board. Their purpose is to create opportunities for residents to engage with nature and find recreational enjoyment outdoors. The activities of the commissions are funded with property taxes levied by the county, and supplemented by other fundraising.

From this relatively simple idea, unique in the Midwest, Iowa has developed an extensive network of nature facilities. Here are some numbers to give a sense of the breadth of this work. At any given time, 495 people serve as commissioners promoting conservation in the counties. The county commissions employ over 675 people; plus more are hired seasonally. More importantly, in the 70 years of their existence, the counties have created over 2,025 parks, facilities, lakes, trails, and other nature-based sites. County conservation areas occupy 200,000 acres of natural land, representing over one quarter of all the protected public land in Iowa. The range of activities sponsored by county conservation boards is impressive. More than 50 counties have built and operate nature centers offering educational exhibits, meeting rooms for classes, and offices for employees. On an annual basis the counties conduct more than 27,000 different educational activities ranging from nature hikes and outdoor classes to large-scale nature activities, and they manage campgrounds, cabins, boat rentals, and other facilities for public use.

Even with this extensive range of activities, the county conservation system seems to fly under the radar of public recognition. If you ask who is responsible for protecting Iowa's environment and expanding nature related activities most citizens will say the Department of Natural Resources and state parks are the primary source for nature activities. When you consider the structure of the county conservation system, the genius of the approach is evident. They are locally funded, close to and responsive to the needs and desires of residents, and have intimate connections to and awareness of the natural resources and geography of the county. County conservation areas offer ways to identify and engage nature's friends, and history shows they serve as engines of economic development and are critical ingredients in promoting tourism and visitation. A new economic study sponsored by the Iowa County Conservation System reports they account for more than $3 billion in economic output for local economies, with county parks alone contributing over $1 billion. They also serve as a way for locals to collaborate with state parks, wildlife management areas, and federal lands managed by the Fish and Wildlife Service and water facilities of the Army Corps of Engineers, such as reservoirs at Saylorville, Red Rock, Rathbun, and Coralville.

The county conservation commissions directly serve residents through nature-based education. The centers provide opportunities for residents, in particular schoolchildren, to access nature, whether through outdoor classes, tours, outdoor excursions, and other nature activities. Many counties with larger populations employ naturalists who conduct regular year-long activities.

In recent years the most important innovation for conservation boards has been efforts to expand funding for land acquisition and new facilities. This takes the form of local nature-based bond issues.

Under Iowa law, the County Board of Supervisors can place on the ballot referendums for residents to vote to increase property tax levies to bond for activities like investing in parks. In the last decade, several counties have proposed and passed bond referendums to fund nature. In 2015 for example, Polk County residents passed a $50 million bond issue for conservation initiatives. The success of the program in expanding facilities led the Polk County Board to place a second bond issue for $65 million before the public in 2023. The popularity and value of the proposed activities helped secure passage with 83% voting for it, including support from the local taxpayers organization. In 2024, Story County residents promoted a $25 million bond issue for nature, which passed overwhelmingly with 78% approval. In eastern Iowa, residents of Johnson County enacted their second nature bond in 2024, authorizing another $30 million for nature.

The key to the success of local nature bonds? They rely on planning by local nature advocates and county officials to specify uses for the funds. The nature campaigns typically list specific projects to be funded so voters know what to expect. Counties have been able to implement the activities, so voters can see the results and be confident the new funds will be spent as promised. The overwhelming votes to approve the nature bonding initiatives show that Iowa's citizens are hungry for more nature protection and are willing to tax themselves to obtain it. The dollar amounts are significant, but when it comes to acquiring land and creating facilities, the average cost to homeowners and taxpayers is relatively small, given how low interest rates are for bonds. A key opportunity is helping additional counties pursue bonding for nature initiatives.

It is heartening to see local voters generating access to tens of millions of dollars to use on specific projects, to implement well-planned initiatives addressing priorities in their counties. In the years ahead the key test will be whether more counties join the effort. There are many regions where this could happen, counties where nature-based activities are driving economic development and creating regional identities like Dallas, Hamilton, Webster, Marshall, Dickinson, Winneshiek, Scott, and others. Although the idea of nature bonding is most often thought of for larger, and wealthier populated counties it is important to remember which county was first to do so. My home county of Adams, with the smallest population in the state, now fewer than 3,800 people, last decade passed a $5 million bond initiative to build cabins and facilities at the newly created Lake Icaria. This foresight and action demonstrate that size isn't necessarily a key factor; instead planning, organization, education, and motivated citizens are the source of power for local conservation.

## THE IOWA NATURAL HERITAGE FOUNDATION: IOWA'S NATURE UNIVERSITY

Look at a map of nature opportunities in Iowa, and one bright spot immediately appears—the extensive network of recreational trails created over the last 40 years. Iowa has more than 900 miles of recreational trails, most on former railroad rights-of-way that became available when rail lines were abandoned. The Iowa trail system did not happen by accident. It was created only through hard work, vision, planning, and funding by many individuals, organizations, and governments. Two groups in particular play a leading role in Iowa's trail success. As you might expect, the county conservation boards, the actual physical location of the trails, play a leading role and often serve as the owners and managers of the trails once constructed. For expertise, leadership, and vision, especially in the formative years of Iowa's trails system, the Iowa Natural Heritage Foundation was the main champion and driver. This happened through the work of Mark Ackelson, then head of the INHF, with the assistance of staff members like Lisa Heins and Andrea Bolton.

The visionary role played by the INHF often involved stepping in to acquire the rail corridor before it was broken up to be sold. The INHF then patiently held on to the property until local communities and counties could identify funding and support to construct a trail. The legal authority to do so is found in the federal rail banking law, a result of efforts by the INHF and other groups urging Congress to act. Now when a railroad decides to abandon a segment of rail line, it must notify the government, which then identifies groups that will acquire the corridor, banking it for possible future use. This step prevents rail corridors from being dismembered. Most trails in Iowa, especially those of any distance, were subject to INHF action.

Iowa's trails provide a perfect vehicle for thinking about nature. They provide natural diversity, illustrate creativity, require local support, and have been created through flexible forms of fundraising. In many ways the trails are a nonpolitical, nonpartisan activity, thriving in a political world by effectively crossing political lines. They involve collaboration between neighboring counties, and because they are hyperlocal, they respond to individual needs of communities and landowners.

Trails are created to connect—people with nature and communities with neighbors. But trails are not like land and water. They don't just exist—instead they have to be created. In that regard they are in and on nature but they exist only through human action. They are an excellent example of recycling land and nature. They provide opportunities to reuse rail corridors, many created in the early years of statehood in the post-Civil War era. Such corridors often contain relatively pristine natural remnants like prairies. It is hard to imagine how you could design a better nature feature for public use than converting rail corridors to recreational purposes. Consider these factors:

They are linear and cross various landscapes, often along rivers and streams.

They are narrow so don't require large acreages to be effective.

They are naturally vegetated scenic corridors, often shaded by trees and provide habitat for birds and wildlife away from roadways.

They are preexisting so don't require negotiating for or purchasing new lands.

They are connective, as railroads always served the next town 6 to 8 miles away.

Unlike long uninterrupted historic trails, like the Appalachian, rail trails make evening walks, short hikes and rides with towns on each end more possible.

Iowa's trails provide opportunities for distant connectivity. The next generation of trail work will focus on trail connections, filling in the links between nearby trails, creating opportunities for more adventuresome trips. Many long loops available in the Des Moines area make it possible to bike for more than 100 miles on protected trails and never repeat the same mile.

The idea of connectivity is playing out in the idea of integrating Iowa's trails into the transcontinental Great American Rail Trail being planned and constructed from coast to coast over 3,700 miles. More than 450 miles of the trail will cross Iowa, and over 250 miles of the trail are already complete here.

Now consider these factors:

Trails are cumulative. Once built they don't get lost, instead usage increases, public acceptance builds, and surfaces are often upgraded and new miles added.

Trails create identity for towns and regions, serving as rallying points for fundraising and special events.

Trails can be funded from multiple sources, including user fees, county conservation dollars, state appropriations such as REAP grants, and even federal funding and congressional earmarks as well as private and corporate sponsors.

Trails create focused projects, giving local groups and organizations such as the INHF a natural topic to promote. Creating rail trails led to the formation of the Rails to Trails Conservancy, a national land trust promoting trails at all levels.

Trails are health affirming—through exercise, time spent outdoors, and connecting with nature—meaning they help fuel public support and happiness. This makes trails perhaps the single most valuable natural feature for promoting health.

Finally, trails serve as economic drivers for new businesses and enterprises and in many situations help revitalize local communities, bringing people and pocketbooks to small towns. The High Trestle Trail with its scenic bridge over the Boone River north of Des Moines is a great example of how connecting trails can spur new businesses and community growth. In January 2025, the Iowa Bicycle Coalition released an economic impact study showing that bike trails contribute over $1 billion in economic activity to the state, which now has more than 80 bike shops alone. Who could have guessed the bikes we rode as kids 60 years ago would have grown into a multi-billion dollar industry! Iowa's recreational trails serve the public in so many ways. They have undoubtedly become the unheralded backbone of Iowa nature.

Thinking about this book as a journey, the idea in my original working title *The Road to Hamilton*, helped me understand how my involvement in and perspectives on nature have been built through my work with the Iowa Natural Heritage Foundation. My work with it started even before I joined the board in 1991. My first project in the late 1980s involved a study on how Iowa drainage law might affect the required closure of agricultural drainage wells under the 1987 Groundwater Protection Act. The concern was that closing drainage wells without available surface drainage could create wetlands crossing onto neighboring properties. One goal was to determine if new USDA programs like the Conservation Reserve Program and what became the Wetland Reserve Program could assist Iowans in closing these threats to groundwater quality. The project was a great example of how INHF staff, here Duane Sand, were always thinking creatively about how public programs could be harnessed to protect natural lands and advance the INHF mission.

Many observers know of the INHF through its land protection work. Our land work is vital, but in my opinion the key value of the INHF lies in cultivating and educating nature leaders for Iowa—landowners, board members, staff and interns. The history of INHF began 45 years ago with the vision of early leaders like Bob Ray, then Iowa's governor; Jerry Schnepf, the first executive director; Bob Buckmaster, Ann Fleming, Dan Krumm, and other business leaders like the Young family of Waterloo. This visionary group believed Iowa needed an organization to fill the role government could not—being nimble, flexible, private, and focused on nature protection. Its key mission would be stepping in to secure land when the public could not act or needed time to generate support or funding.

Their vision was inspired, and the organization has spent four decades identifying and cultivating a community of landowners and stewards willing to protect their land and even donate large tracts for Iowa's people. In many ways the Iowa Natural Heritage Foundation functions as Iowa's Nature University. Having spent 50 years in the university setting, seven as a student and over 43 on the faculty (in many ways I never left school) it is natural for me to see its work through this lens. Consider how the INHF operates like a university: training leaders, employing faculty, building and caring for facilities, recruiting students, educating the general public, and fundraising to support its work. In everything it does, the INHF is focused around the broad curriculum of nature, with nature serving as the ultimate educator. The value of its work is apparent across Iowa. You need to look no farther than Iowa's hundreds of miles of bike trails. Nearly every mile of a bike trail located on an abandoned or former railroad corridor involved the INHF.

What started as a two-person shop, with the first major success protecting the 1,000 plus acres in the Mines of Spain south of Dubuque, has grown into a powerful engine for nature. Today the organization has over 30 full-time staff, a board of directors of 36 volunteers from across the state, and dozens of college students employed each year as interns working on the mission. The financial picture is strong—donors and board members have invested in securing an endowment to support the work. The most important measure of the INHF's work is the over 200,000 acres of Iowa land now permanently protected in more than 1,600 projects.

You no doubt contribute to charities, so you know one way to measure their impact is to look at how money raised is spent, how much for administration, how much for fundraising and how much on mission. If an organization can keep its administrative expenses below 20%, then it is well run. Alternatively, if a large percentage is spent on fundraising this is a serious red flag. By these nonprofit metrics, INHF has an incredible record, spending over 95% of its annual $20 million budget on projects with only 3% on administration and less than 1% on fundraising. Numbers like these give its 12,000 members and donors a real sense their money will be used for the mission and spent wisely.

The well the INHF draws from is Iowans need for nature, a well with few limits. Consider the range of our nature needs:

protecting and restoring lands;

improving public access to nature with parks, trails, and wildlife areas;

protecting wildlife habitat across the natural world, from pollinators to endangered bats;

planting and restoring prairies, with seed harvests like the one pictured below, and prescribed burns;

helping daylight oak savannas, freeing them of undergrowth blocking the sun;

protecting Iowa's unique landforms like the Loess Hills, Iowa Great Lakes, the Driftless, Mississippi River flyway, prairie potholes and rolling southern hills;

improving Iowa's water quality and resisting the forces degrading it; and finally

protecting Iowa's fertile soils and the rich farmland sustaining our agricultural economy and rural culture.

All these elements are the work of Iowa's Nature University. They require several things: expertise on the faculty; living examples to demonstrate what can be done on the land; staff, students, and volunteers willing to do the work; donors and members willing to write the checks to advance knowledge and understanding; and public institutions and officials who understand the value of the work and assist where possible and stay out of the way when necessary. The final ingredient is a welcoming public, eager to engage with nature and ready to be recruited for the mission. All these elements combine to make the Iowa Natural Heritage Foundation uniquely suited to be Iowa's Nature University. The goal of any university is to help its students find hope for the future. The search for hope is the topic we turn to next.

## I Lost Another Friend

As the professor was finishing the book, news came the world lost a visionary leader—Pope Francis. I hope you realize, regardless of your religion or lack thereof, I lost a great friend too. No world religious leader in modern times—no make that perhaps in history—since the time of his namesake St Francis of Assisi, has spoken as eloquently about the role of nature—me—to human life, and encouraged people to take regard for me in their actions. In his Encyclical Letter, Laudato Si' issued May 24, 2015, Pope Francis reminds the world I am our common home and there is an urgent challenge to protect me, to enter "a new dialogue about how we are shaping the future of our planet." He notes, "we need a conversation which includes everyone, since the environmental challenge we are undergoing, and its human roots, concern and effect us all." Over the following 90 pages Pope Francis provides a comprehensive, nuanced, and powerful statement for how humans must embrace their responsibility and love for me. If you have not read it or perhaps even heard of Laudato Si', I encourage you to find it—there you will read the words of a true friend of nature. May his words find support in the hearts and minds of all people.

## Chapter 8
# Where Is the Hope? Nature Summits, Education, and Water Quality

My favorite way to enjoy nature is walking. Doing so every day helps me stay healthy and find time to think. Large parts of this book were composed out on a hike, with notes jotted down for later deciphering. I mark each day's mileage on my calendar, then tally it up by week and month. For 2024 it was rewarding to reach a daily average of 6.9 miles, at least according to my iPhone, and to have the year come in at 2,618 miles, a nice bump from 2,372 miles in 2023. Yes this may seem a little borderline OCD, but as habits go it is better than chewing your nails.

You have caught hints that trails are a favorite topic of mine. Nothing brings me closer to nature than walking a beautiful path. The photo below shows one of my favorites, walking down the eastern slope from the mission at St. Inez in Solvang, California, a favorite winter

getaway. What is most telling about this photo is if I hadn't told where it was taken you might have guessed anywhere in the world—the French countryside, a North England jaunt, the Italian hillsides. The trail reminds me of what Jason Isbell sings in *Cumberland Gap* "if you don't sit facing the window you could be in any town." Nature's beauty awaits us anywhere we care to look.

For many years my heart has been set on walking the Coast-to-Coast Trail in the United Kingdom. Just thinking about the 190-mile pathway from the Lake District through the Dales connecting farms, villages and the countryside makes my mind wander. The hike was going to be my reward for turning 65 and then for each year since. Turning 70 was finally going to be the magic number, an epic walk to mark the milestone, but it didn't happen. No doubt you too have experienced this reality, setting goals on the calendar months ahead that often get overtaken by events on the ground—illnesses, pandemics, new gardens to plant. This year may be different, at least I hope so. After putting this book to bed, that is handing it off to Steve, my publisher, the plan is to do a nice bit of nature hiking. If I can locate a good companion to join me, a not unreasonable condition set by my wife, it might even be to the UK. If not there, maybe I will explore the pieces of the LoHi! Someday efforts to knit together the existing segments of the LoHi trail stretching the length of Iowa's Loess hills will be complete, offering the opportunity to hike this unique Midwestern landform. Either way, hopefully by the time you read this, my hiking advaenture will be history, ask me how it went if you see me at a reading.

Finishing this draft, I read Ian Frazier's *Paradise Bronx: the Life and Times of New York's Greatest Borough*. I am a longtime Frazier fan, and have read most of what he has published. His ability to weave history and personal insights into his travels and the places he visits makes him one of America's most valued authors. Toward the end of *Paradise Bronx*, he writes about the concept of mutual aid, one of the important strengths he encountered in people living in the Bronx, the people driving its recovery. The reference made me think about how the concept of mutual aid is a valuable insight for thinking about our relationship to nature and to our future. Frasier describes mutual aid as, "a movement that encompasses the core values of building and sustaining community." Mutual aid is not charity, not an organization and not an agency; instead it is a practice. He continues, "mutual aid starts with the recognition our bodies are intertwined, that we depend on one another. This means we are not some individualized self-sufficient beings; on the contrary we are radically inter-dependent." It is hard to put into better words a description of our relationship to nature than saying "we are radically inter-dependent."

## LOOKING FOR HOPE: THE IOWA NATURE SUMMITS

We have discussed many examples of how nature is threatened here in Iowa and the U.S. However, you can see we are not without reasons for hope. This chapter highlights several developments benefiting nature—places, projects, and people creating hope for a brighter nature future. The most important starting point is all of us, the citizens who care about nature and are looking for answers. When you consider the range of nature opportunities we have and the number of people involved, it is clear nature has many friends and perhaps a much greater capacity for leading us to better policy and projects than we realize. In many ways the premise that nature has many friends waiting to be tapped was behind my organizing the Iowa Nature Summits.

I set out the idea to hold an Iowa Nature Summit in *The Land Remains* as one of the big ideas we need to consider. Traveling the state I saw that we had a broad and deep body of people working to protect nature and no shortage of organizations devoted to the work. However, when I considered the political issues, water quality, funding, or the hot potato of acquiring public land, history showed me the friends of nature were always on our back heel reacting and waiting for the next bad idea from the legislature, one we would have to fight. I concluded that we needed an opportunity for people and organizations involved with nature to come together, to take stock of our skills, and to plot a better course. Some observers noted this was nothing more than speaking to the choir. My response—When was the last time we ever got the choir together? Certainly not in my lifetime.

In many ways the stories and success of the 2023 and 2024 Iowa Nature Summits have proven the value of bringing the choir together. Rather than singing solo we are joining the power of our voices to sing in harmony. Planning and organizing the first nature summit was a rewarding experience. Receiving positive responses from over 50 nature organizations from across Iowa to sponsor and help promote the summit proved that interest was there. By the time the first summit took place in November 2023, interest was so strong we actually had to turn people away. Over 300 citizens attended, hearing from dozens of speakers committed to working across the range of nature issues. They were shocked to learn the recent news Iowa has the second highest incidence of cancer in the nation. They were excited to learn about nature-based educational initiatives like the School of the Wild program operated by the University of Iowa College of Education. In planning the summit we made a concerted effort to be sure younger voices were in attendance.

We are proud to offer scholarships so students and others can attend and we will so again for the 2025 Iowa Nature Summit in November.

In many ways the summits show the value of focusing on local issues, on land-based projects, to encourage people to move their communities forward. Many of those attending the summits are leading such efforts. Certainly national political swings can effect local efforts, but locally driven initiatives led by community volunteers are harder to stop or reverse. The wisdom of working with local groups is reflected in the success of the Iowa Natural Heritage Foundation and the donations of land made by the friends of nature. These organizations and people illustrate how energy and passion can coalesce to benefit nature. The point is if you are looking for hope there are projects and organizations offering it. We just need to look for them and elevate and magnify their efforts.

Making connections is a vital theme of the summits. Connections can be physical links, like the new Athene Bridge connecting Raccoon River Park in West Des Moines to Walnut State Park across the Raccoon River. This connection and the trail links make it a valuable addition to the Des Moines nature scene. Connections can also be psychological, linking us to an idea, purpose, a political movement. Here are five ideas for actions those who attended the summits were asked to consider taking.

First, we need more connections to nature. The great news is the opportunities to increase connections with nature already exist. Think of all the nature-based organizations in Iowa and the wide range of outdoor activities they sponsor. Taking advantage of these opportunities is a key step toward making connections with nature and to find hope, adventure, and fulfillment.

Second, join an organization. This might involve writing a small check or a larger one if you can. The size is not as important as the act of doing it. The power of philanthropy is immense, not just in what it can accomplish for those on the receiving end but in the satisfaction it can bring the giver. When you become a donor you make an investment in the organization and its cause. You also make a statement about your values and priorities, about what you identify as being important. This is one way to invest in nature and our future.

Third, consider volunteering your time and energy to promote nature. There are countless ways to do this from joining a river cleanup, like project AWARE, to going on a prairie hike and seed collection, organizing a neighborhood cleanup, or just carrying a trash bag on your daily walk. By volunteering, you will have the opportunity to be out in nature and you will most likely be sharing time with others who love nature. Volunteering with an organization lets you see how your work can help further its goals.

Fourth, we all have the opportunity to learn and care about nature. There is so much to see and do and learn about Iowa nature. From history to taxonomy, from identifying prairie plants and birds to learning how healthy soils create healthier foods, all these and more are part of our ongoing relation with nature. Nature is a patient teacher, and its classroom is always free and open to give us unlimited opportunities to learn and to grow.

Fifth, consider caring and then acting. As we learn about nature and engage with it in any of the many avenues available, we increase not only our understanding but deepen how we care for nature. Caring is a first cousin to love. Caring for nature makes our connection with it come full circle.

## NATURE-BASED EDUCATION

One valuable source of hope for nature in Iowa is expanding nature-based education. The concept is simple: create ways to engage students in learning about nature and get them hooked on it. School gardens are one example of nature-based education that have been promoted for several decades. The premise is straightforward—have children plant seeds, tend plants, grow crops, and ultimately harvest them for use in classrooms and lunchrooms. School gardens have been widely embraced as a creative way for children to learn about nature. They are often promoted from a health perspective, as championed by famous chef Alice Waters with her Edible Schoolyard program, developed in Berkeley and now found across the nation. Promoting school gardens was at the heart of efforts by Curt Ellis and colleagues who founded the Food Corps, a national youth service initiative. I had the honor of helping bring Food Corps to life 20 years ago and am impressed how it has grown. In addition to educating tens of thousands of elementary students in school gardens managed by Food Corps service members, the program has trained hundreds of college graduates to become advocates for healthier food and better nutrition policy. Many are now employed in this important work as teachers, administrators, and advocates.

Another type of school garden initiative is the use of seeds, nature's original small-scale education miracle. Herman's Garden from Seed Savers Exchange offers schools and educators packets of heirloom vegetable and flower seeds to use in planting school gardens. An important way to educate children about nature, school gardens are just one example of how schools can become nature's classrooms.

If the land is available, there are many ways to demonstrate how nature works and engage children in hands-on learning—constructing rain gardens, building wetlands, and even planting prairies. One exciting nature education effort featured at the Iowa Nature Summits is the work of Mark Dorhout in the Panorama School District. He helps the district maintain a 20-acre prairie next to the school, and during the course of the year he engages every fifth and sixth grade student in projects involving the prairie. Each student even constructs their own bird house. There is hardly a subject for which outdoor activities in the prairie can't be employed—science, math, geography, history—everything can be touched by what is growing.

The School of the Wild, operated by the College of Education at the University of Iowa, is another valuable initiative. Many people first learned of its existence by attending the summits. The program began 25 years ago to serve students in Iowa City schools. As awareness of the program grew, other schools asked to be included. The decision was made five years ago to expand the program statewide. The idea is to engage fifth and sixth graders in a week-long immersive all-day nature-focused curriculum. The University of Iowa enjoys free access to nearby Lake Macbride State Park and more than 480 acres of natural lands owned by the Army Corps of Engineers, the Macbride Nature Recreation Area. These natural lands stretching between the Coralville Reservoir and Lake Macbride offer the perfect setting for the School of the Wild. As the initiative has expanded to other schools, teachers often partner with county conservation boards to use local nature facilities. Schools can work with organizations, sports groups, and individuals to solicit volunteers to teach the curriculum. People who love nature typically enjoy the opportunity to speak to school kids and share their passion. The value of the School of the Wild has helped it obtain financial support from groups like the Iowa Wildlife Federation.

## Nature on the University of Iowa, Decision on Macbride

Wouldn't you know it, no sooner had the professor written this paean to the wisdom of the University of Iowa—his alma mater—operating the School of the Wild than word came that University officials are considering an action greatly complicating its future. The issue is the long-term 30-year lease the university has with the Army Corps of Engineers giving it free access to the Macbride Nature Recreation Area. The university is considering not renewing the lease, allegedly because of costs associated with maintaining the property. This was kept fairly secret until local friends of nature got wind of it and spread the word. Interested parties were invited to submit comments to the president and a study committee she formed. No surprise, the professor sent some pithy ones and has given me permission to share portions of them here:

"I am writing for several reasons—first as a 1979 graduate of the College of Law I have a strong interest in the actions of the University. I came to Iowa after completing my degrees in Forestry and Economics at ISU, and had the honor of serving as a research assistant for Dean Hines for two years. While at Iowa I visited the Macbride field campus on many occasions—as did many of my colleagues. After leaving Iowa I began my long career teaching agricultural law and have been with Drake now for over 40 years where I created our Agricultural Law Center. Much of my life has been devoted to teaching and writing about the land, nature, and conservation. This is why it is important to speak out in opposition to any decision the University might be contemplating to end the lease with the Army Corps giving your staff and students access to the MNRA. I know you are hearing from many Iowa alumni and residents who feel the same way—and I have been encouraging people to contact you.

"One activity we have sponsored through the Center is to create the Iowa Nature Summit—our first was held in November 2023, the second last October, and the 2025 Summit is on Nov. 19 and 20th. A topic featured at both Summits—and will be again in 2025—is the School of the Wild program run by UI Wild through the College of Education. As I hope you realize this program is one of the most innovative nature-based education programs being operated by any school in the nation. It is just one example of the unique and innovative opportunities available to the University through the use and access to the MNRA. Given the growing importance of the environment, nature, climate, and related issues—as well as the related health benefits associated with access to nature, it is hard to understand why or how the University would be seriously considering severing the relation with the Corps for the Macbride. Most Universities would be ecstatic to have access and proximity to this gem of nature.

"I am certainly aware of the challenges Universities are now facing with the disastrous shift our nation has experienced with new political regimes and extremists in charge at the national and state level. The disdain being shown to higher education and the values which for generations have underpinned the ideal of knowledge is heartbreaking. The financial pressures you face are daunting. But as you realize, we in higher education—and nature—need to take the long look, confident this shift in society will be short lived and the pendulum will swing back. When it does Universities who had the wisdom and foresight to stay the course, to continue commitments to long term programming—like what you are able to do at Macbride—and who avoided temporizing with fiscal decisions they come to regret—will be hailed for their courage—and supported by their students, faculty, and alumni. One bright spot and opportunity presented to the University by this challenge is the ability to reach out to collaborate and seek partners among the many other nature organizations in your area—most notably the Johnson County Conservation Board. The University and Macbride have many friends who are anxious to help secure your future, please don't hesitate to seek their assistance."

Well, those are interesting comments if I do say so myself. But the professor saved the best for last and even brought me into the fight for Macbride. Here is how he ended. By the time you read this book, we will know the outcome.

"I am in the final stages of editing my third book—*Through Nature's Lens*, which will join *The Land Remains* and *The River Knows*, as my trilogy reflecting on land, water, and nature in our state. The Back 40, a field on my childhood farm in Adams County narrated the Land, and the Raccoon narrated the River. This book is narrated by Nature and there will be a passage concerning the University's decision about the Macbride. I hope—and nature hopes—the discussion will be positive and hopeful rather than a sad review of a bone headed action forced on a proud University by short-term pressures. Good luck with your decision. I and thousands of other Iowans are anxious for the news of your decision. Prof. Neil D. Hamilton" PS: Update, July 2025—bone headed won, lease will end in 2029.

## OTHER NATURE-BASED EDUCATION ACTIONS

Nature-based education offers a vehicle for colleges and universities as well as nature organizations, to collaborate on projects offering educational benefits and real gains for the environment. For example as part of its mission the Blank Park Zoo in Des Moines has a broad commitment to nature education. One innovative project it has developed involves new technologies and cooperating landowners to help propagate the population of Blanding's turtles, one of Iowa's endangered species. The following description from a zoo press release explains it:

The project began in April 2022, when the Iowa Department of Natural Resources (DNR) reached out to Blank Park Zoo to help combat the decline in Blanding's turtle populations across the state. The zoo, in collaboration with the Iowa DNR and Iowa State University, embarked on a mission to reverse this troubling trend.

To make the project a success, Iowa DNR works with public and private landowners to create and manage habitats needed by Blanding's turtles. Iowa State University uses radio-telemetry to manage turtle populations on public and private land to determine population size on a local scale. When Iowa State University finds pregnant females they are brought to the zoo to start the head-starting process. This process includes X-rays to locate and identify eggs, inducing the female, incubating and hatching, and rearing the turtles until they become big enough to relocate back to where the female was found. The female turtles are returned to their original habitats after they lay their eggs by Iowa State University.

After two years of work to find viable eggs, four turtles provided a total of 57 hatchlings this year. The hatchlings will be cared for at Blank Park Zoo until they are old enough to be released into the wild, contributing to the population's recovery.

"This accomplishment is a major win for our conservation efforts and highlights the effectiveness of our collaboration with the Iowa DNR and Iowa State University," Anne Shimerdla, President & CEO of Blank Park Zoo said. "The Blanding's turtle desperately needs these kinds of successes to ensure its survival. We are proud to play a role in this vital conservation effort and look forward to seeing these turtles thrive in the wild."

The zoo's work with Iowa State University and the Iowa Department of Natural Resources to help ensure the future of Blandings turtles is a wonderful example of what is possible through collaboration. But you don't have to be a teacher or a zoo to connect children to nature. If you have ever taken a child outdoors to camp, fish, or bird watch, you know how powerful and rewarding the experience can be. If you don't have children you can borrow some from friends. This is my wife's approach. One of Khanh's favorite summer activities is collecting monarch caterpillars from the garden, raising them on milkweed leaves, watching them form their chrysalis, and waiting for the butterflies to emerge. The picture below shows a newly gathered group of caterpillars chomping away on milkweed leaves.

Over the years many friends with school-age children have had the experience of coming to the farm to see the process, even helping release the butterflies in the garden. Several have even taken caterpillars home to raise themselves.

There are many key values associated with nature-based education. First, it gets kids outdoors where they can be active. It offers many avenues for learning and can be integrated into almost any subject. Second, it connects children with other living things, helping build empathy and understanding. Third, it creates a way for kids who may not shine in other areas, like sports or academics, to reveal hidden talents to their peers. Think of the country kid who excels at fishing. Fourth, nature-based education creates lasting memories. Children may not remember what happened in a math class, but they will remember seeing a family of bluebirds nest in the house they built or watching a butterfly emerge from the chrysalis of a caterpillar they collected in the prairie. Nature programs can spark special interest and connections. Consider the many times you have heard success stories about professionals who when asked "how did you get a start," answered, "it was in a class when I was 10 years old and we did" you can then fill in the blank with their favorite nature activity. Fifth, the programs can engage other volunteers in the community, conservationists, and scientists happy to share time and knowledge with youth. Connecting kids and adults can break down age-based misperceptions in both directions. The programs are flexible and versatile, meaning teachers can use nature however they want—whether in history, math, science, culture, or art. Sixth, the programs give children the opportunity to put their hands in the soil. Getting dirty connecting with reality in this way is an important change from sitting inside clicking on a device and staring at a screen.

Nature-based education can stimulate children's imaginations and offer ways to encourage creativity. Challenging kids to design their garden plot, choose their plants, harvest their vegetables, and select their recipe gives them a sense of responsibility and the satisfaction of watching their ideas come to life. Yes, there are challenges to using nature-based education: the time involved for teachers, the possible costs, whether there is sufficient interest, continuity for maintaining a garden year round, and available administrative and institutional support. How the programs relate to evaluation criteria for education can also be a question. These challenges are real but not insurmountable, as the many successful nature programs show. As the value of nature-based education becomes more widespread and appreciated and as more training opportunities for teachers are created, being able to integrate nature into our educational system will become more possible and expected.

One reason nature-based education is so powerful is its human dimension—how it builds on our optimism for the future. We don't often think about the fact death awaits us at some point. Instead, we live for today and the years we see ahead. We plant seeds, till gardens, and educate children. We plant trees knowing we may never sit under their shade. The idea of planting trees came to me when visiting New York City in spring 2024. I took a long walk up the west side of Manhattan to visit Hamilton Grange (facing page), the home he built and lived in for the two years before his untimely death, maintained as a national memorial by the National Park Service. One interesting fact I learned at the Grange, when Hamilton had it built he planted a circular grove of 13 poplar trees, one to represent each colony.

Returning to Sunstead, I was inspired to create my own version. Several summer days were spent tracking down trees to plant in the front meadow. Rather than choose 13 of the same species, I planted 13 different trees ranging from horse chestnuts to river birch, from red-

Hamilton Grange
National Memorial

National Park Service | U.S. Department of the Interior

bud to lindens, and more. Who knows, this summer I might expand the mini-arboretum by planting another set of trees, perhaps eventually adding one for each of the 50 states. If you plant a tree, the shade of which you will never enjoy, I guarantee that one thought will come to your mind—why didn't I do this 20 years ago?

My Hamilton-inspired tree planting reminded me of taking several seedlings home to plant on the farm. It was summer 1974 and the seedlings were from a forestry project in my studies at Iowa State. Today, 50 years later, the larch and a nearby yellow birch are thriving, though the farmhouse is long gone. The larch and yellow birch are possibly the only specimens of their type in Adams County. Here is a fun forestry fact lodged in my mind from school days. If you scratch the inner bark from young yellow birch twigs, you will be struck by the evocative and identifiable scent of wintergreen.

## MORE SOURCES OF HOPE FOR IOWA NATURE

One of the most important examples of hope and transformation in Iowa's nature picture is the Iowa Confluence Water Trails—or ICON project in central Iowa. The premise behind ICON is simple: harness the rivers flowing through our capital, the Des Moines and the Raccoon, and use them to provide recreation and outdoor activities for Iowans. What began over a decade ago as a vision for using the rivers has progressed toward completion. Over $100 million has been raised from private sources, government grants, and other funding streams. Improvements on the Scott Street dam will provide fish passage and a recreational whitewater course. Related projects at the Harriet Street kayak takeout and a new project on the Raccoon east of Fleur Drive, next to Gray's Lake and the Kruidenier Trail, will create exciting water-based activities for people of all ages and skills.

ICON shows how transformative developments begin with a big idea and how one person can drive a dream forward. Many people are involved with ICON and the new vision for our rivers, but Rick Tollakson stepped forward from his position with Hubbell Realty to provide the leadership, support, and energy to get the project moving. His connections in the Des Moines business community validated the project, and his organizational energy created the team of volunteers, consultants, engineers, and city officials necessary to make it happen. The supporters persevered, the plans matured, and the early fundraising success provided momentum as the project took shape. What many people originally pooh-poohed as simply a pipe dream that could never happen is actually happening! ICON has the potential to be the most significant natural resources project in central Iowa since construction of the Saylorville dam over 50 years ago.

One important challenge faced by the project is water quality. A common criticism has been, why spend so much money putting people into the rivers, knowing they are often polluted? This is not an entirely unreasonable thought, although the fact that water may be high in nitrites doesn't make it unsafe to paddle in, as might high bacteria levels. However, if you take nature's long look and focus on connecting people to nature, you can see how ICON may be just what is needed to help push Iowans to deal with water quality. The more people connect with nature and use the rivers, the more political support is created, with more citizens and voters expecting policies to support cleaner water. Seen in this light, ICON is not just a recreation project, it is a major step forward toward creating a healthier balance with nature.

## Nature on PFAS and Sewage Sludge

Howdy, nature here—you haven't heard from me for a while. Sorry to intrude on the professor's hope fest, but let me throw a stink bomb into the crowd. If you think some of my comments about how you treat me have been too harsh, then what am I to make of the newest insult you have delivered? You know, the twins of PFAS—forever chemicals—and their first cousin, sewage sludge. The issues are somewhat different, although both show your attitude toward me—dump your wastes, literally and figuratively, on me, assuming I will "remediate" them for you and the public, no questions asked, no responsibility expected. PFAS are a relatively new concern, one you finally came to recognize, once you finally got around to asking, what if the chemical you so willingly considered benign really aren't? Benign is such a handy word, one you often use to describe things you may not really understand.

Now lo and behold, you have discovered the dangers are real. Instead of being benign, in many cases the ubiquitous PFAS may be malignant, with significant and as yet not fully understood health risks for humans, animals, and the soil and land where they have been applied. The name was a dead giveaway—forever chemicals! It is not clear how you now expect me or anyone to remediate them. The fact the PFAS controversy is now emerging raises two issues. First, those who don't believe in science or who find its conclusions inconvenient will have time to invent conspiracy theories for why PFAS really aren't dangerous, or if they are why no one can be blamed. Perhaps your Solons of justice in the legislature will even try to enact immunity laws so that manufacturers and users of PFAS can escape liability. This is your second line of defense—the MAGA types who don't believe law should advance justice or protect the public if it costs businesses money. They have time to develop legal strategies to avoid liability, perhaps taking a playbook from the Bayer Roundup bills to use legislation to establish some much needed legal insulation.

The second issue concerns the land application of sewage sludge. It is related to the PFAS problem because the sludge may contain them, along with the heavy metals people always knew were being concentrated. One difference between sewage sludge and PFAS is no one concerned about health or the environment ever really believed land application of sewage sludge was entirely safe. Science recognized that heavy metals could accumulate in the sludge removed from your turd rollers.

But what can you do with the millions of pounds produced each year—it has to go somewhere! Why not just dump it on me! Your idea is as old as time—slather it on the ground, plow it into my fertile soils, and then call it a fertilizer or a soil conditioner or whatever label makes you feel good. Maybe you can even get farmers and landowners to pay for it! Now that is really genius! Municipalities have a waste product they need to get rid of as inexpensively as possible, so why not turn it into a product? Your favorite citizens—the entrepreneurs—can always develop a business model to relieve you of your problems, for a reasonable fee of course. Then they turn around and presto the dross becomes gold—a marketable product! Remember, the professor already explained how markets work—product, buyer, seller, price, and a marketplace and you have it all! Funny that no one ever thought to label sewage sludge as an ecosystem service. Maybe people always assumed this wouldn't turn out well—just like my fish who to their surprise sometimes find a hook in the worm.

Now you have something else to worry about, so just get in line. This won't be so easy, though, for the farmers and landowners who discover that hundreds of acres of their fields are contaminated. Finding this out can mean the crops grown there such as the grass they had hoped to feed their dairy cows to produce milk can't be used or the products will be unmarketable. I imagine by now the lawyers among you are already contemplating the lawsuits among cities, landowners, sludge slingers, and others trying to sort out who may be on the hook for damages. Once the lawyers get involved, as they are now, some will no doubt say that the ones to blame are the government officials and businesses who started it all. When will you ever learn that I am more than a convenient dumping ground for your wastes?

# A Few Thoughts about Water Quality in Iowa

Previous chapters have made it clear that water quality has a long history in Iowa and presents significant challenges surrounding what to believe and whether we are making progress. I have given many presentations on Iowa's water quality over the years, views summarized in these conclusions, five reasons why Iowa has failed—so far—to address problems with water quality.

First, we aren't really serious about it. There are many projects and activities underway, but it is hard to argue in good faith we have come to grips with the serious and endemic nature of water-quality issues. Worse, we are poised to repeat the same patterns of denial and deflection. We can't even be honest with ourselves about any progress we are making. Consider cover crops, a practice many agree can improve water quality. It is good news cover crop use has increased in Iowa, but in 2024 state officials made the outlandish claim we have now planted 4 million acres. If you actually drive around rural Iowa you might wonder where they are hiding, because cover crops do not appear to exist at anywhere near this scale.

They probably don't. The 4 million acre estimate is based on a methodology of asking randomly selected agricultural retailers to survey customers for their impressions of cover crop use in the area. This handful of surveys was then extrapolated to obtain the 4 million acre estimate. Rather than use available satellite imagery to identify the actual acres planted, we chose to promote an inflated guess. Our approach is like visiting a health club to ask regulars to estimate what percentage of people have similar exercise habits. A second example concerns a favorite water-quality practice: saturated buffers along streams. Iowa State promotes buffers claiming they can remove up to 40% of the nitrogen moving in the water. Unfortunately, recent research measuring the efficacy of saturated buffers indicates the nitrogen removed may be closer to 7%. This significant difference in the utility of the practice hasn't stopped Iowa from promoting saturated buffers under the "batch and build" approach to deal with water pollution. You can see the challenge.

Second, water quality is contentious because it may require us to act. We may need to identify who and what is to blame, assign responsibility, consider remedies, and make changes. We are not eager to do any of these, so we keep our distance and periodically explain why we just need more time—and why regulations won't work—even though we never try using them.

Third, we fail to address water quality because the state doesn't have a clean water plan for Iowa. It is not the much touted Iowa Nutrient Reduction Strategy, a plan designed to reduce pollutants we put into the rivers and send down to the Gulf of Mexico. This is not a clean water plan for Iowa, and it is not clear that if it is ever achieved we would know the difference. Can you tell if the stream you are paddling on has 40% less nitrite in it? Neither can I.

The nutrient reduction strategy is an exercise in magical thinking about farm-based pollution, the largest source of pollution, because the plan is entirely voluntary. It asks and requires nothing of the farm sector to reduce pollution of our waterways. Early in 2025, the state announced a new version of the plan, buying time going forward. The new plan includes encourageing farmers to diversify crops using a four-year rotation, with two years of alfalfa rotated with corn and soybeans, to reduce nitrogen use. Crop rotations are a historic way to diversify production and reduce nutrient needs, but does anyone really believe Iowa corn producers, facing declining incomes and increasing demands for ethanol, are going to plant large acreages of alfalfa simply to deal with water pollution? You can add dreaming to the plan's magical quality.

Fourth, Iowa has difficulty addressing water quality from agriculture because of the nonpoint source pollution exemption in the federal Clean Water Act. This exemption, created for political rather than scientific reasons, essentially insulates crop producers from any potential restraints to protect water. Our water-quality problems will not go away, and more likely will continue to get worse as a result of the relentless push to increase yields, to raise more corn to produce more ethanol, as discussed in chapters 4 and 5.

Fifth, we are not making significant progress improving water quality because the public is not adequately engaged or enraged. When we fail to question why water pollution continues and who is responsible, the problems grow worse. Surprisingly, this point makes it possible to find what could be glimmers of hope. Iowa may now be nearing a tipping point in acknowledging the impact of farming on water quality. The recent fertilizer spill on the Nishnabotna and the controversy over the cattle feedlot on Bloody Run Creek have increased public attention to water quality. Public alarm over rising rates of cancer are triggering new questions and concerns about the causes. As 2024 ended, the Biden EPA took the unprecedented step of ordering Iowa to add segments of several major rivers—the Des Moines, Raccoon, and Cedar included—to the list of impaired waterways under the Clean Water Act. The EPA based its action on studies showing rivers used to provide drinking water, are clearly contaminated with nitrites from fertilizers. The state resisted the action, not because it disagrees, but because it does not want to restrict future point source users of the rivers by having to create the total maximum daily load plans required once a river is listed as impaired. Only time will tell if this EPA action is another one set for reversal.

Given this long history of challenges with water quality, you may wonder whether it is possible to find hope for significant changes in our future? Part of my hope rests in the next chapter—the concept of justice and a belief that we share a commitment to justice as a societal goal. Identifying injustices, like those we are inflicting on our water, can be a needed motivation to help us reconsider how we use and abuse natural resources. It is said the arc of the moral universe may be long but it tends toward justice. I believe the same is true about the arc of dealing with Iowa's water quality. The timeline may be long but is bending toward hope. I am not alone in this belief. Many Iowans share my belief—and you may as well.

James Larew, an environmental lawyer who helped form the Driftless Water Defenders, believes the issue of environmental justice to protect water quality is Iowa's next civil rights movement. We all know the fight for human equality and respect is still an ongoing struggle, but we are (or were) making progress. It is difficult to predict what events may be tipping points to change public attitudes and bring progress, like someone refusing to sit in the back of a bus. We have seen several symbolic events with nature and the environment in our nation's past. The famous incident of the Cuyahoga River catching on fire crystallized the issue of water pollution in the 1960s, as did publication of *Silent Spring* in changing our views on pesticides. Today the image of a lonely polar bear swimming in an ice-free Arctic has come to symbolize the threat of climate change. The question is, what will be our image for Iowa, our tipping point? You might suggest a photo of a stream full of dead fish, but haven't we already seen this photo many times? Perhaps it will be the headlines concerning Iowa's cancer incidence? No one can predict when the tipping point may be reached, when the statute of repose may give way to the avalanche of change, but hope is what keeps us watching.

Nature is patient, certainly more so than we. Once our lives play out we die, whether we have reached our goals or not. Nature continues. What it can hope for is our support during our lifetimes. It is our obligation and responsibility to pass the torch so that the search for justice is handed to those who come next and the journey can continue. Searching for justice for nature—and ourselves—is our next subject.

# Chapter 9
# The Search for Justice: Who Speaks for Nature?

Responsibility and justice are both critical to our future and to nature's future. Responsibility flows from the ideal of an ordered society, where citizens and government share a commitment to each other and to a sustainable future. Justice is the goal and measure of our success in creating that society. Our embrace of social responsibility is the essence of citizenship—an opportunity and an obligation we ignore at our peril.

What does Justice mean in the context of Nature? We all have a right to expect that laws will be enforced and the tools of justice employed, including the wise use of regulations to protect nature. One goal of public policy should be to limit further deterioration of natural resources by protecting prairie remnants and stopping the wasteful destruction of grasslands, timber, and wildlife habitat. Laws should not be used to inflict damage on nature or protect bad actors from the consequences of their acts. Today, Iowa's laws can inflict harm—right to farm laws privilege hog lots over neighbors, regulators place pipelines over property rights, and political compromises like nonpoint source exemptions shield water pollution from remedy.

Sadly, some people worry that it is too risky to speak of justice because listeners might take offense. Having spent over 40 years teaching about justice, I don't agree. Justice is not something to fear—instead it is the basis of hope. Those who fear justice may do so because they benefit from injustice. Justice is about preserving opportunities, about valuing and hearing all voices, and about expecting government to function. We all have our own internal sense of justice, and each of us knows unjust conduct when we see it.

Unfortunately, we don't often ask what is unjust, but if you take a moment you can develop a list. Here is an example: Iowa's "no role for regulation" mantra is inherently unjust. Giving individuals unlimited freedom to act without fear that the public will set reasonable expectations for their conduct is unjust. It ignores the proper responsibility of government to protect the public welfare—and nature—and instead shifts the burdens and costs to individual citizens, expecting them to perform the responsibilities being shirked by public officials. This disenfranchises citizens, especially in rural areas, and perverts and ignores the rule and role of law.

Justice is not a shackle but a beacon. The real shackles—the ones we experience every day—are the shackles of conventional wisdom, the dogmas telling us what to think and what questions we shouldn't ask. Consider the "truths" we are expected to embrace as Iowans:

Corn and ethanol are the economic future. We can never have too many pigs. We cannot afford more parks, trails, and wildlife areas. We don't need science or data to tell us how to monitor water quality because—trust me—it is getting better.

I could go on—but so could you. Our challenge is recognizing how these shackles of conventional wisdom, the truths we are told to accept, are often not truths but instead just rationalizations to protect the economic determinism dominating our state. These view nature—our land, soil, water, and wildlife—as simply a storehouse free for the looting, without restraint and with little regard for the public. We know other, better truths. The Iowa Tourism Office brags about the billions in economic activity tied to nature and the outdoors. Business leaders say how critical nature is to growing the workforce. We hear about the many lands being protected and the efforts of individual landowners and groups to restore prairies, create wetlands, and embrace wildlife habitat. It is an injustice to ignore these truths.

Our challenge is not just to confront actions we find unjust—as hundreds of Iowa landowners are now doing with the misuse of eminent domain to support the pipeline boondoggle. Our responsibility is to stand up and offer an alternative path, one recognizing and valuing nature—one understanding how nature contributes not just to our enjoyment and fulfillment but to all dimensions of society. You understand this responsibility or you wouldn't be reading this.

We are nature's advocates. Our job is to confront injustice, to defend and define nature, and to offer our voices and experiences to elevate and celebrate nature. Turning to the question, Who speaks for nature?– the answer is we do—all of us, the groups you belong to whatever their size and shape. It is our responsibility to share our critically important voices for nature. This is a grand exercise, an adventure we share as collaborators and cooperators for a healthier Iowa nature.

## THINKING ABOUT FREEDOM AND HOW WE SEE NATURE

We all love freedom; it is a value and goal we share. It is at the heart of our democracy and legal system. Some believe that the thirst for freedom explains why many oppose regulations. Andrew Bacevich in *Age of Illusions: How America Squandered its Cold War Victory*, makes a powerful statement about freedom when he notes that "employed as a rationale for policy, freedom possesses a surprising elasticity. It can justify almost anything, it prohibits virtually nothing."

Bacevich illustrates this idea with a 1756 Edmund Burke quote, "The great error of our nature is not to know when to stop" and thereby ultimately "to lose all we have gained by the insatiable pursuit after more." These two powerful forces reflect our attitudes toward nature. The lack of limits allows us to use land and water—nature—free from any responsibility of regulation or public good, while shackled to the conventional wisdom we love the land and are feeding the world. Combined these forces drive our soil, water and climate issues. We accept no limits on our freedom and never know when to stop. Rules to protect nature however, don't mean the government is coming to take your land. Instead, the rules help ensure that you do not take away the rights of other citizens to enjoy nature. When John F. Lacey said in 1901, "the immensity of man's power to destroy imposes a responsibility to preserve," he knew this was a responsibility we owe our children—and nature—to embrace.

Iowa has a new state motto—Freedom to Flourish. I may be alone, but isn't this just a dog whistle to the MAGA crowd—at its heart an antipublic, antigovernment code for elevating markets and economics over society? Isn't it fair to ask where the Flourish part is—or is all the emphasis on the Freedom? If we are to flourish, rather than brag the state has a multi-billion dollar surplus and race to find new ways to cut taxes and underfund needed public services—like denying additional summer food assistance to feed children—why not use the opportunity to address matters in desperate need of funding? Think of what Iowa could do with a small fraction of this surplus: fully fund REAP, monitor water quality so the University of Iowa doesn't need to hold bake sales, replenish the DNR budget so state employees can fulfill their duties, and support county soil conservation districts to assist landowners in protecting water quality and improving soil health. These steps would actually help Iowa flourish if our leaders cared. There is no reason to believe farmers will not embrace treating their farms as ecosystems if they have support and market alternatives to do so—to flourish! The key issue often missing in our discussions of freedom is how we ignore the other side of the coin—responsibility. Real freedom carries with it responsibility to society and to other citizens. Freedom by itself is just another word for anarchy.

People threatened by the ideas in this book, fearful their ability to use nature will be restrained, often characterize concerned citizens as simply a bunch of nature lovers. We are people who like to play outdoors while they are trying to make a living. This is a dangerous mindset because if political issues involving nature are reduced to choosing between Iowa's pigs and playing in the river, history shows the pigs win every time—at least so far. Respect for nature is about much more than just enjoyment—as vital as that is. Respect for nature focuses on the essential role—the foundational role—nature plays in supporting life. Without nature there is no human survival, it is that simple. This is why water quality, soil health, and climate are essential to our future—why we need to elevate the importance of nature in our advocacy.

If we want the view of nature in Iowa five years from now to be better, not just a continuum of little progress and slow decline, changes must be made. How do we get out of the rut—the ephemeral gully—we find ourselves in today? One important question is, Who speaks for nature in our state? Even though many citizens find hope in nature, we lack a unified voice speaking for nature. This is in contrast to the constant, amplified voice coming from agriculture and industries like biofuels. The proliferation of nature groups means their positions are often resource or activity specific—think prairie enthusiasts and paddlers—and their organizations are limited in size. Having no overarching body to speak for nature leaves a gap in advocacy that forces some groups by necessity to play a larger role than their missions may suggest.

This asymmetry means that when an issue arises, such as the regular and outlandish claims of success on water quality made by the Iowa Secretary of Agriculture—such as on the 10th anniversary of the Iowa Nutrient Reduction Strategy—there was no unified voice presenting the other side—nature's side—of the story. Instead, as is usually the case, Iowans were treated to a one-sided echo chamber from those happy with the status quo, while the voices of nature were mostly silent and unorganized. This is dangerous for nature's advocates—especially now with the extremists in charge at the federal level, when we can expect frontal assaults on public lands; on funding for wildlife areas; and on support for anything raising the issue of climate change.

So what can we do? There are many steps to take. Some things are clear: Iowa needs more collaboration, more cooperation, and better communication among nature groups and we need to build on the many connections we all share. These are reasons why creating the Iowa Nature Voters is well worth considering. We need to be more assertive in our defense of nature and more strategic in our advocacy. The failure of Iowa's politicians to fully fund the REAP program at $20 million a year—let alone the $35 million needed to account for inflation is a disgrace. Instead, REAP has been level funded at a measly $12 million for many years, putting the lie to the claims we are doing all we can to protect nature. Fifteen years after Iowans voted overwhelmingly to create the Natural Resources Trust Fund—and still no funding—is just as disgraceful. By failing to raise the sales tax we have missed out on investing over $2 billion to improve water quality, protect soil health, expand wildlife habitat, and increase recreational opportunities. There is widespread agreement among Iowa's nature organizations and citizens of the need to support Iowa's Water and Land Land Legacy—IWILL—and raise the sales tax to fund the trust. But as I wrote previously, the Iowa Farm Bureau asked its loyal supporters in the legislature to propose a bill to begin the process of repealing the constitutional amendment before it receives a dollar! Thankfully the nature community rallied to quickly defeat the proposal. Who knows? Maybe the effort at repeal will serve as a wakeup call to spur real action.

We are too willing to accept minor victories, a tract of land protected here and there and bad legislation that didn't pass, at least yet. We are too easily brushed off and told to be patient. If the reward for our patience is a failing Nutrient Reduction Strategy, deteriorating soil health, an underfunded DNR, and a refusal to protect water quality as seen with the failure to punish those responsible for polluting the Nish, then there is really no reward.

What does being "Iowa nice" get us, if those who see nature as an obstacle to their profits are happy to continue abusing it at breakneck speed—and expect public approval and funding for their work? There is no reason to expect improvements without a fight. Fredrick Douglass reminds us that progress does not come without struggle. It is foolish to think that hopes for nature in Iowa will ever be achieved without conflict or controversy—or through voluntary acts alone, the magical thinking underpinning the Nutrient Reduction Strategy. No one gives up power voluntarily. I have said many times that Iowa needs more truth tellers and fewer happy talkers. Positive changes are possible, but we need to ask hard questions about the reality we face.

## THE RELATIONSHIP BETWEEN JUSTICE AND NATURE

In thinking about the relationship between nature and justice, I turned to an expert whose writings about land have helped shape my understanding of the environment and the operation of our legal system, in particular our relationship to the land. In his book *After Nature: a Politics of the Anthropocene*, Jedediah Purdy presents his thinking about the history of our conservation and environmental movements. Purdy frames his analysis around the idea of imagination and how "law is the circuit between imagination and the material world. Law choreographs human actions in a thousand ways." He notes history reflects four periods of conservation thinking: providential, romantic, utilitarian, and ecological. Each of these eras of development shaped the history of Americans' use of our natural resources and our politics. Historically we thought of nature as being before or without politics, but now we understand how politics shape nature. This is a large part of what has changed about our new era, one where we face at least three crises: ecological, economic, and political.

As our discussions have shown and as Purdy concludes, we can't avoid the role of politics in our efforts to address these issues. In doing so, we are essentially making political choices. This is one reason why relying on markets by themselves will not provide answers, because as he notes, markets cannot avoid political choices both to create and to assign values. His point is that "widely held, strongly felt views for how we value nature are sometimes necessary conditions for new laws to govern nature in new ways." This history of imagination and choices underpinning the nation's lawmaking regarding nature has been true from the time of John Lacey and the Antiquities Act until today. Purdy concludes, as you have read previously, that our new politics of nature will need to be based on the concept of responsibility for what we make and what we destroy. His reminder that our choices and actions are a function of imagination is important for understanding how democracy, our ability to decide our future, continues to play a critical role shaping the future of nature.

What is nature's future? Here are some questions to consider.

How do we expand citizen science and engagement? River cleanups, water-quality monitoring, prairie seed harvests, and field days all illustrate this potential. The more opportunities we create and the more we engage citizens will help build a broader political constituency for nature while doing good.

How do citizenship and civic responsibility shape this work? Just as we share a right to nature, we also share a duty to protect nature. It is not someone else's responsibility. If we care, we need to act. One responsibility is to prevent legitimizing inappropriate uses of land through technology. Just because our equipment is bigger is no excuse to plow up pastures and just because generous tax subsidies are available, pipeline boondoggles don't need to be approved. Who decides what is "appropriate" is a key question at the heart of all environmental debates. The answer: society must decide what is appropriate, not just the marketplace. We never ask, What is nature's standard for determining when an action is appropriate? If our technology or laws allow us to do something, drain a wetland or plow a prairie, does that mean we should? Is the only calculation the potential economic gain, or should we weigh nature's future and our children's future in our decisions?

What role can nature play in local politics? Protecting nature usually does not play out well before county boards and city councils. We understand that nature is not a luxury—but the reality is most local policies, like zoning, community development, and school curriculums, are not built on concern for nature. Instead, the key driver is economic development and profits. If nature is considered at all, it is as an add-on, something to be afforded only if there is extra money or someone complains loudly enough.

This is why passing county nature bonds are so important and inspirational. In the last decade, Polk County supervisors gave citizens the right to vote on and approve over $115 million in two bond issues so the County Conservation Board could fund nature—and it is not alone in county nature bonding. The recent votes in Story and Johnson counties show that local governments can harness public support for nature if they have the courage. The University of Iowa's School of the Wild demonstrates how every Iowa school district can help children learn about nature and collaborate with local nature groups if they have the vision and willingness to do so. Let's encourage them!

What is enough when it comes to nature and land protection? If the premise is we can never afford to protect all the nature we need, the debate becomes simply a question of what we can afford and support for nature becomes a fight for funding among competing priorities. This approach is ill-conceived. Personal duty and responsibility for conservation cannot be premised on the view "I will do as much conservation as the public pays me to do and only that." This is the recipe for failure reflected in our voluntary-only approach. Similarly, public support for nature shouldn't be only if we can afford it.

The question isn't, When is there enough nature? Instead the real question is, What does nature need? The answer is simple. Nature needs us to change our attitudes so that more landowners, citizens, and politicians will care about nature's future. Public programs can be designed to support nature. Funding the Natural Resources Trust is a good place to start; as is fully funding the Resources Enhancement and Protection Act. Land doesn't need to be owned by the public to be protected. Landowners can protect their land at any time, if they desire to. Some believe that the distance we need to travel to change minds to protect nature is too great and the cost even greater. In my view, changing attitudes on how we view our responsibility to nature doesn't need to carry any price tag. The distance we need to travel is only a few inches. It is all in our heads and in our hearts.

## WHAT DO WE GET BY COMBINING JUSTICE AND NATURE?

What happens when we combine a focus on nature with a respect for justice? As to justice, the important questions are: how do we access it, what does it mean, and if used as a lens to examine nature's place in society what does it tell us? We can agree that nature is a relatively benign, nonpolitical idea—who is against nature? The trouble starts once you ask what supporting nature will require from us? If it means trying to elevate nature's needs to being equal to or even above those of humans, you open a can of worms.

If we can agree that nature is nonpolitical, then can we also agree that justice is nonpolitical? Who can be opposed to justice? Like nature, the trouble may begin when we try to define what justice means as it relates to human conduct, especially when we try to decide when actions are unjust? The key question is: What can we gain by combining a concern for nature with a concern for justice? I believe we can define justice by considering actions we can all agree are unjust.

We all have an internal sense of justice, one we have understood since childhood. Not being allowed to go outside to play when others were allowed to hurt our feelings, an indicator of the injustice we felt. Thinking about what we find unjust can help us define what is just. To illustrate the idea of how defining justice can be added by identifying injustice, I asked Nature to share its thoughts about what it may find as unjust in our state. Here are twelve examples Nature identified.

## Nature and the Idea of Injustice

First, limits on nuisance suits restrict the property rights of neighbors, all done in the context of enacting right to farm laws favoring agriculture over others.

Second, landowners are allowed to tile, plow, bulldoze trees, and take many other nature-degrading actions with essentially no limitations at the expense of nature.

Third, private companies can be given the right to use eminent domain for private projects over the objections of landowners.

Fourth, your Iowa Supreme Court has abandoned the role the courts should play in evaluating legislative actions and administrative decisions, degrading public resources and hollowing out the public trust doctrine.

Fifth, local governments defer to land development and resources use, for example by defaulting to approve all annexations, granting all water use permits, and failing to adopt even minimal regulations to restrain private activities.

Sixth, Iowa's soil conservation laws offer the appearance of legal authority, but in reality local elected soil and water conservation districts have no funding, no staff, little respect, and limited ability to influence landowner conduct.

Seventh, Iowa law fails to prevent the use and loss of prime agricultural land for other developments, such as the server farms gobbling up thousands of acres of prime farmland in central Iowa.

Eighth, state and local programs do not require testing of private wells placing thousands at risk of drinking unsafe water.

Ninth, Iowa fails to fund effective water-quality monitoring or support local citizen water-testing efforts.

Tenth, the "no role for regulations" mantra in Iowa law shifts responsibility to individuals, meaning you expect private citizens to police public authorities, effectively relieving these officials from any responsibility to implement or enforce regulations

Eleventh, Iowa has no state environmental advocate authorized by legislation or recognized by the courts to speak for me, which limits any recognition of my rights in Iowa.

Twelfth, the nonpoint source and point source distinction in the Clean Water Act exempts agriculture from regulation but places significant burdens on point sources. This creates the absurd result a rural resident could pay thousands to install a septic tank, while a multi-thousand head hog facility built across the road would face little expenditure for a waste-handling system.

## CITIZEN JUSTICE

In the post-WWII period, perhaps no person is more identified with what would become the modern environmental movement than Justice William O Douglas. When I was a young law student and bud-ding environmentalist, reading Douglas' *Go East, Young Man* offered insight into his early life, filled with activism, passion, and its share of controversy. As a wunderkind in the Depression years from his position on the Yale law faculty he championed the efforts of President Roosevelt to use legislation to address the nation's ills. He took his talents to the Security and Exchange Commission; appointed as a commissioner in 1936, he fought for a legacy of progressive safeguards. Roosevelt nominated him in 1939 to join the Supreme Court at the age of 40, making him still the second-youngest justice ever appointed.

Douglas's long career on the bench was marked by the brilliance of his opinions, the creativity of his legal ideas, and his willingness to pick a good fight. His emergence as a leading voice for protecting the environment was notably connected to his efforts in the 1950s to protect the C&O Canal stretching northwest from his home in Georgetown along the Potomac River to Cumberland, Maryland. The C&O Canal had fallen into disuse but continued to exist, becoming a naturally wooded pathway. Douglas regularly hiked the canal way on weekends as a convenient link to nature and to the river. The fight over its survival came to a head when plans were announced to use the corridor to build a highway. Joining with conservationists and others concerned about the loss of this historic landmark, Douglas picked up the fight to preserve it. Most notably he challenged the editors of the *Washington Post*, who had editorialized about the need for the highway, to join him walking the corridor to see firsthand what it had to offer. His challenge was accepted, and what followed was a classic Douglas creation: strenuous daily hikes; politicians, boy scouts, and other officials joining for segments; great food and drinks in the evenings; and lots of publicity as the delegation hiked the 190-mile trail. By the time the hikers reached DC the Post's editors had changed their mind, and over the next few years the forces came together to preserve the trail as part of the National Park System. This challenge epitomized Douglas's strategy for protecting nature—political activism, strenuous outdoor activity, and constant publicity. As the National Park Service notes, the C&O Canal was the first national Park ever "walked into existence."

His work on the C&O reflected Douglas's belief that advocating for nature is a right of citizenship and a responsibility we all share. He didn't believe either of these duties stopped just because he had been named to the nation's highest court. Over the decades to follow, he well earned the title Citizen Justice as he worked to help protect nature, civil rights, and so much more. In doing so he galvanized a coalition of the friends of nature, setting the foundation for what would become our modern environmental movement. In her book *Citizen Justice: the Environmental Legacy of William O Douglas, Public Advocate and Conservation Champion*, M. Margaret McKeown details both the canal walk and his career. If you ever take the Capitol Limited train to DC, the C&O Canal path can be seen out your window as you travel in from Harpers Ferry.

Justice Douglas' commitment to the idea that advocating for nature is a right of citizenship is reflected in several ways today in Iowa. Perhaps most notably it can be seen in the recent creation of the Driftless Water Defenders. This group has come together to protect the natural resources of the Driftless region in northeast Iowa. The ongoing fight to protect Bloody Run Creek in Allamakee County was a precipitating event for its creation. Local residents, trout fishers, and others concerned about nature believe the state has unnecessarily and illegally threatened the future of Bloody Run by approving an 11,000-head cattle feedlot just a few miles from its headwaters. One of only a handful of Iowa streams designated by the state as "outstanding waters", Bloody Run is home to a naturally reproducing population of trout. These facts didn't prevent the Iowa Department of Natural Resources from awarding a permit for constructing and operating the feedlot. The Driftless Water Defenders challenged the permit as a violation of Iowa rules protecting groundwater in this region of karst limestone topography.

Several legal actions have ensued, including a successful challenge to the first manure management plan the DNR approved for the facility, requiring the plan to be rewritten. A second and perhaps more significant action was a fight over the state's decision to grant a water withdrawal permit to provide the millions of gallons needed to supply the feedlot. After a lengthy trial and an almost 10 month delay, an administrative law judge in December 2024 issued an advisory opinion. He ruled the department had not followed Iowa law for granting a water permit by failing to consider the possible environmental impacts of such a permit. The DNR argued it never takes environmental concerns into consideration and instead only determines if sufficient water is available to satisfy the request. In January 2025, the DNR again granted the water permit, explaining that providing water for livestock is vital to the state and noting it had addressed the judge's concerns. The Driftless Water Defenders have challenged the decision in court, leaving open the question of what might come next for the feedlot and the water permit. What is clear is one development: the formation of the Driftless Water Defenders.

Several well-known Iowa environmental leaders lead the organization, including Chris Jones, author of *The Swine Republic: Struggles with the Truth about Agriculture and Water Quality.* Jones is perhaps most famous for the controversy over his departure as a water-quality scientist at the University of Iowa. That departure, initiated in part by pressure from "concerned" legislators, shares a sad lineage with the Bloody Run permits. Both involved questionable ethical actions, conflicts of interest, and base political motivations. Joining Jones is Larry Stone, an award-winning environmental and conservation reporter. For decades, he was the voice of nature, writing for the *Des Moines Register.* The third leader in the effort is James Larew. Jim has had a long career in Iowa politics, his environmental work has focused primarily on representing citizens challenging environmental actions of large industries, meaning he is willing to take on entrenched entities. He is an eloquent speaker on behalf of nature. Perhaps his most poignant perspective, one he often shares with Iowa audiences—is his belief the fight to protect water quality is the next civil rights struggle for Iowa.

The Driftless Water Defenders is a prime reflection of Justice Douglas' brand of activism, but the organization is not alone. In several other situations recent Iowa environmental controversies have led to coalitions and groups of citizens joining to protect their interests, stand up for the rights of nature, and challenge the political hegemony dominating official decisions in our state. As discussed in chapter 5, Summit Carbon Solutions' proposal to sequester carbon by building a pipeline to pump liquid $CO_2$ to North Dakota has generated significant opposition. The proposal is perhaps the most significant example of how Iowa's official attitude towards nature reflects a willingness to sacrifice it if it promotes the interests of our current system of agriculture.

Not unlike the Bloody Run feedlot situation, the outcome of the legal fight over the pipeline is not concluded, but both examples offer many lessons. One is the importance of local citizens coming together to raise concerns about a problem affecting nature in their own backyards. A second is rather than simply complaining, the real source of potential solutions, power, and satisfaction for concerned citizens comes when they take action. Providing an opportunity for people to express their concerns, come together to share them, and unite in some form of joint action to seek relief, whether in the courts, at the ballot box, or in the street is justice for nature in action. These are the hallmarks of citizen justice and if he were alive today Justice Douglas would undoubtedly be a member of the Driftless Water Defenders, fighting for the future of Bloody Run Creek. He would oppose using an archaic pipeline technology to convince ourselves we are doing anything significant to address climate concerns. Instead, Douglas would argue we should directly confront the actions contributing to climate change, rather than construct a Rube Goldberg-like invention, funded by taxpayers to fool ourselves into believing we are doing good work.

## THINKING ABOUT AGRICULTURE, RELIGION, AND JUSTICE

Reading Kristin Kobes Du Mez's thought-provoking book *Jesus and John Wayne: How White Evangelicals Corrupted a Faith and Fractured a Nation* helped me understand one dimension in the history of how we got where we are today in our search for justice. It revealed an essentially unknown world, at least for the nonreligious and perhaps even for regular Christians, about what has become the Christian nationalist movement. I mention this movement because it includes at least two important connections to how we think about nature. First is the theme of domination—how many humans believe all of nature is by definition subject to our control, meaning the only role for nature is to yield to our desires. Second is the role of militancy and violence in defining this idea of religion. Consider how this theme is revealed in the language of war and violence so embedded in our modern agricultural system. If you don't agree, watch the next TV advertisement for a pesticide and listen to how it will vanquish the enemy. This militarization of farming may help explain why sustainability faces challenges. Is it too feminized and doesn't reflect the control and domination needed by "modern agriculture?" By advocating for nature in a way that supports getting along and compromising, sustainability may not fit the image agriculture wants to project.

To plow, to till, to drain, to poison, to fence out, to eliminate pests and wildlife—these are all variants and values of the domination theme. To confront these ideas do we as nature's defenders need to soften our approach? Or can we just create something new to fight? Why not go to war and fight soil loss and fall tillage rather than fighting nature as we do now by killing weeds and bulldozing trees? The failure of our pest control approaches, such as planting millions of acres of Roundup-ready crops, comes from overreliance on the products, and leads to resistant weeds. This leads us to develop newer, harsher forms of chemicals such as dicamba, all while nature is working 24/7, selecting for heartier and hardier pests who will resist our newest poisons.

This pattern shows two things. First is our hubris in thinking technology will dominate nature, rather than accepting the wisdom of working with it. Second, denying the reality nature is working 24/7 means its resilience will continue to defeat our efforts. All the while we waste our natural fabric in the form of soil health using chemical intensive methods. The damage to insect populations from the overuse of neonicotinoid seed coatings is just the latest example. Our answer always seems to be to substitute even more industrial products, such as nitrogen, to make up for our failing technologies. The reality is we appear both foolish and wasteful at the same time. Some faithful rationalize this because the Bible and God tell us we should dominate nature. The voices of the faithful who note the biblical ideal of stewardship or those who have taken to heart the words of the late Pope Francis, appear to be in the minority. Either way, we must recognize all the stewardship in the world won't get us justice.

## Nature Reconsiders the Impact of the 2024 Elections

Previously I said that elections are not a major concern to me. At the same, time I can't look at what is happening with your new administration without a real sense of sadness. Not so much for me, I will survive or at least most of me, even with the drumbeat of "drill baby drill" and the vindictive and senseless, let alone economically wasteful, efforts to roll back anything referring to climate or even clean energy. My sadness is for you, certainly for the friends of mine who have worked so valiantly to protect me and elevate my needs. You must realize that all the people working on issues of environmental justice, are really working to benefit me, as they seek to lessen the burden of environmental harm to the communities and people you have long been willing to ignore. My sadness extends to those so gleefully wielding chainsaws, slashing funding, and swinging sledgehammers to destroy programs and institutions. How did they become so hardened, so deluded, so vain and self-centered? Little do they realize the nature and social bonds they strive to dismantle were established for their benefit and protection, too. Drinking unsafe water is a risk to all, as are breathing dirty air, and consuming pesticide-laden food. Perhaps they believe their politics and red hats will prevent the hand of fate, often delivered in the doctor's diagnosis, from landing on their doorstep.

So, yes, I am sad and dismayed, disgusted even at what I see unleashed in your nation. Take, for example, the senseless and vindictive action—at least to me—of killing a major assessment of me that had been underway for several years. In February 2025, the full draft of the first *National Nature Assessment*, just a month from completion was terminated. The decision came in one of the now infamous executive orders. This meant the work of over 150 scientists and experts and thousands of hours of effort might be shelved. Why? The White House didn't really say—or feel an explanation was needed, though observers note the assessment includes a chapter on "Nature and Equity in the U.S." I hope that the many experts and institutions involved find the courage and the funding to complete and publish the Assessment, as they promised to in reports about the effort to cancel the study. From my perspective, having their detailed assessment of my health and your opportunities will be a valuable tool for us to use when this current tempest passes, as it will.

My solace—and eventually yours, or the solace of those who come next—is my knowledge and faith in our resilience and my hope that your politics will eventually be self-correcting. The overreach we are seeing is just that. As the prices being paid in the damage to me and the threats to your health and future continue to be revealed, the pendulum will swing back. When it does, I will be here waiting patiently, perhaps a bit tattered and torn but still resilient and resurgent never the less—and still happy to welcome my friends, old and new.

# Chapter 10
# Nature's Future: Charting a Course for Action

In the early stages of writing this book, thinking it would hinge on all things Hamilton, one topic was to be the famous Hamilton watch company. Unless your name is Waltham, Elgin, or Bulova, you might not know the pleasure of wearing a fine watch with your name on it. Not surprisingly, wearing Hamilton watches was a family tradition, and my parents gave me a beauty for college graduation. Unfortunately it was lost years later in an incident with the infamous sailboat, described in *The River Knows*. Khanh replaced it and over the years has given me several more. My Road to Hamilton research included going online to learn about the company and see what was out on eBay as to Hamilton watches. It was either a costly mistake or an exciting adventure—perhaps both as the photo below shows. I returned to my senses and the Hamilton focus was dropped, but it was a great excuse to add to my watch collection!

Collecting: now here is an American trait for you. We collect everything and have affinity groups, newsletters, magazines, even whole cottage industries to support our various afflictions or addictions, depending on your perspective. If you are at home, please look up from your reading. Can you spot evidence of your own collecting habits—books, artwork, and figurines? In my younger professorial days when I travelled to Europe regularly to lecture and teach, a must-do before coming home was to find a new Hummel figurine to bring my mom. By her untimely death 25 years ago—beware falling down the stairs in an old farmhouse—she had a shelf full of goose girls, young boys, and all the other familiar Hummel scenes. Cleaning out the farmhouse after she passed meant boxing them up, so they now reside tucked away somewhere in our basement. Their value may be small, but the pleasure they brought to my mom was worth every dollar spent.

We satisfy our needs to collect in many ways. Some are physical like my watches and my mom's Hummels, others take the form of experiences and memories. This is one way nature helps make our lives complete. Think of the travels you have taken, visits to national parks, cruises to Alaska, and how often nature was at the heart of your decisions where to go. Now it fills your memories and photos of what you did there. We have many reasons to value nature, to protect and enhance it, but making sure that it will be there to be the storehouse of experience and memory for ourselves and for those who follow is as good a reason as any.

## Fools, Politicians, and Distractions

One of my amusements is watching your human antics. I especially find pleasure in the foolish and often ridiculous ideas of politicians. No surprise, the ideas often involve me—

like trying to deny scientific realities. News Flash! You cannot control the weather regardless of what a congressional savant may think! There have been some real high points in the Political Fool Olympics in recent years. One proposal sure to medal was offered by a young Iowa senator, a Republican if you must ask. In January 2025, speaking to a national conference of people involved with marketing farmland, he proposed, possibly in all seriousness, that the state of Iowa purchase the bottom tier of nine counties from Minnesota, for a price to be determined. He opined the landowners residing there would enjoy the lower taxes offered by Iowa and the farmers would avoid the onerous regulations Minnesota forces on them. You know, outlandish ideas like requiring buffer strips along rivers and streams to protect water quality and stricter regulations on livestock facilities and manure disposal. It appears the audience and news reporters weren't quite sure whether to applaud or laugh at the statesman's idea. I just shook my head and sighed, as no doubt the old professor wanted to as well—the senator was another one of his former law students. For all the times people labeled him a pinko trying to indoctrinate his students, the professor doesn't appear to have had much success, even after taking class loads of students to Cuba!!

Speaking of Olympians sure to win gold in both the foolishness and buffoonery categories, the winner will no doubt be your new president, the Fool-in-Chief. In fact, he could sweep the field and win the trifecta if allowed multiple entries! Buying Greenland for show, making Canada the 51st state, and renaming the Gulf of Mexico, after only 500 years of history, the Gulf of America. You can throw in taking control of Gaza as a bonus! And no sooner had he announced the renaming than your mapmakers, search engines, and agencies—toadying favor or fearing furor, perhaps both—fired up the printing presses to go along. Time will tell if they accept Illinois Governor

Pritzker's February 2025 declaration renaming Lake Michigan as Lake Illinois? If this trend catches on, buying stock in paper makers may be a good market play.

## WHY NO HOLIDAY FOR NATURE?

In late 2024, just as we came off Thanksgiving, with Christmas and New Years looming and Halloween in the rearview mirror, the question struck me, Why don't we have a day of celebration, a national holiday focused on nature, for nature's sake? We have Labor Day, often spent outside but with a definite history to celebrate workers. We have the extended 4th of July weekend also spent outdoors but with a patriotic bent. We have Memorial Day, the official start of summer but with its own purpose to recognize those we've lost. These all touch on nature but don't honor it, at least directly.

Another candidate is Arbor Day, definitely with a nature focus and a history reaching back to the 1870s. As a social event though, it seems to be fading from our culture. My guess is nine out of ten people couldn't tell you when it is (last Friday in April), or why we celebrate it. When was the last time you planted a tree on Arbor Day? The one candidate we have coming closest to being a holiday for nature is Earth Day. This April 22nd event, started in 1970, is often considered the birthday of the modern environmental movement. It definitely has a nature dimension—it is hard to see the earth as anything else—so there is potential here. Perhaps it is just me, but does Earth Day seem to have become overly politicized with a focus only on environmental problems, protests, and looming crises? In some ways it's a casualty of our capacity to turn all environmental issues into partisan watersheds and looming disasters—remember The Population Bomb? This may explain why recognition and promotion of Earth Day events seem to be waning after only 50 years. Do you remember how you celebrated it this year? Exactly. Earth Day is certainly important, but it's not really nature focused or especially hopeful or celebratory—at least not as much as it could or should be.

This raises several questions. Why is there no Nature Day? Does it run counter to a Judeo-Christian hegemony for approving public celebrations? Mother's Day is a no-brainer, but Mother Nature Day, not so much! Does it reflect our attitude of treating nature as the canvas where other acts are painted, rather than as the subject itself? Maybe it is unclear who would propose or organize such a day or what the traditional activities could be. Will there be fireworks, parades, pie-eating contests?

A lack of love for nature can't be the reason—just look around and see how nature is regarded. Certainly there is no shortage of nature-focused organizations; our experience with the Iowa Nature Summits prove that. Similarly there is no shortage of activities we could include on Nature Day. From river cleanups like Project AWARE, neighborhood trash walks, community beautification plantings, and prairie hikes—a wide range of nature activities, already exist. Many are accompanied by the expected 10K run and 5K walk with appropriately designed nature-focused T-shirts and tattoos for the kids! The Des Moines Ikes have an annual weekend Nature Expo providing free fishing for kids, canoe lessons, archery classes, and other outdoor activities. Similar events are found in towns and cities across the land. Maybe all these existing nature activities can be packaged into one great scoop for national Nature Day! This doesn't mean we should stop honoring nature every day instead Nature Day would create an opportunity to reflect on the role it plays in our lives.

When could we have it? Late April seems like a good time. The weather is nice, the ice is out of the lakes, the fish are biting, nature is blooming, and the birds, insects, and animals are awake, hard at work for another year. Fields are being tilled, gardens being planted, streams being paddled. Yes, April is a perfect time for Nature Day. The celebration would follow Easter, itself a nice lead-in to rebirth for those so inclined. And the date would fall before Mother's Day, itself an appropriate opportunity to honor the nurturing role of human mothers everywhere, a nice sequel to honoring Mother Nature.

So here is our challenge, a big idea to consider. Let's put our heads together, select a date, stake a flag, and announce plans for a new holiday, a new tradition in the making. Nature Day!

## Does Nature Need a New Farm Bill?

Nature here and my answer is yes, there are several reasons why I and you can both use a new farm bill. First, the one you are working off of now, at least for me, is essentially the conservation title of the 1985 Farm Bill, meaning it is 40 years old. There were many good ideas in that bill to protect fragile lands: the conservation reserve program, highly erodible land, Sodbuster and Swampbuster. All these provisions transformed America's approach towards conservation. Over time however, the new can fade as a new normal sets in and people adjust their conduct. Time can reveal design problems. Both are true for the 1985 Farm Bill Conservation Title. Conservation compliance, the idea that farmers need to meet conservation rules or lose farm program payments, is a powerful idea. The only problem is the USDA has little stomach to enforce the provisions and agricultural groups and farmers resist, so exceptions are made, excuses are accepted, and the power of compliance is lost. When the Agricultural Law Center conducted a survey several years ago, few farmers or landowners said they fear federal enforcement of conservation rules. In addition, over time it may become clear that some issues haven't been addressed, for example, the need for conservation programs on working lands rather than just retiring land from production. This recognition gave rise to 1990-era programs like the Conservation Stewardship Program and the Environmental Quality Incentives Program widely used today. As a result, the conservation title has come to reflect numerous add-ons developed as the need arose. This contributes to making it a good time to regroup, to take a holistic approach, as you like to say, to design a new farm bill for me.

Second, issues recognized as important challenges now may not have been considered 40 years ago. Climate change is a perfect example (or was), as is the growing need to address soil health—the living parts of soil and not just soil quantity. You also need to consider water quality and how agriculture affects it. Water quality is considered an issue for the Clean Water Act, but the act offers almost no rules for agriculture because of the nonpoint source exception. The extent legislation has addressed climate issues came largely in other forms, like the Inflation Reduction Act, a Covid era spending bill designed to spread funds across a wide range of social issues. The funding and ideas were not developed as part of a farm bill. This helps explains why the new Republican regime in control has largely jettisoned these ideas as it approaches what could be the 2025 Farm Bill.

Third, and perhaps most important, the current farm bill debate, such as it is, has reverted to the old pattern of being all about federal subsidies. Which region and which commodities will be rewarded and how will the money be delivered? Will it be through so-called crop insurance (really a form of guaranteed income for the chosen to the tune of $10-$15 billion a year) or some other form like "disaster" relief? These are questions in the farm bill debate. In all this discussion, my role, largely identified in agricultural terms as conservation, receives little attention. Like spending on nutrition, the other bugaboo agriculture can't escape or eliminate, the idea for conservation is to provide enough funding to avoid being labeled as uncaring but not go too far, that is, providing enough to make a real difference.

These three factors mean your farm bill is an outdated system, not designed for today's needs. The political process of building it has entrenched politicians and farm groups alike. They are cemented to doing things their way, and resistant to change, especially if change might mean losing control or favor. Unlike the intellectual debate and study that went into developing the 1985 Farm Bill seasoned policy experts inside and out of government are largely absent. The USDA has neither the interest in or the capacity to lead any reevaluation; It is happy to shovel money out the door and stay below angry politicians' radar. Farm and commodity organizations are happy with what they have created, especially if any serious reconsideration might threaten the money they receive or establish a new generation of expectations and rules. No one in agriculture is anxious for a new Sodbuster or a serious effort at compliance. Remember: these are the dreaded regulations that agriculture fears like Vlad fears daylight.

The agricultural sector is happy to continue promoting voluntary efforts and "market-driven" ideas like the previously dissected sustainable aviation fuel boomlet. They are happy to promote the false narrative "no-till" farming is a form of resilient agriculture and good for the environment, rather than acknowledge it promotes increased reliance on pesticides in exchange for reducing tillage. Now agriculture leaders have two new fears. One is staying out of the crosshairs from the DOGE cutters, who might look askance at the billions poured into farm programs. The second is trying to survive the economic turmoil of a new round of trade wars against their largest markets.

Where does this leave you? I know where it leaves me, pretty much on my own, hoping for the best and looking for good stewards who take care of the land. As for you, it leaves you limping along doing it the old way, temporizing where you can, hoping the public doesn't get concerned about the amounts being spent, and perhaps waiting until some crisis—natural or of conscience—leads you to change.

## NATURE DAY AT THE IOWA STATE FAIR

The Iowa State Fair is always on my list of must-do activities. It has been this way since I was a young boy, when we would put the camper shell on the pickup and go to the fair. The Clearfield Lions from a town near Lenox have been responsible for driving the tractor shuttles you see at the fair. This meant hundreds of locals set up camp there. Last year I went to the Fair and decided to use nature's lens to see what I could find. The answer was not much! Once you get past the wonderful exhibits maintained by the Department of Natural Resources in the classic brick building near the west entrance, nature mostly disappears. Of course it is there indirectly in the foods of all shapes and flavors, mostly fried, you can buy. And it is there in the displays of farm equipment and livestock exhibits. When it comes to anything celebrating our rivers and streams, our trails and parks, our fertile soils and grasslands, there however is little to see or appreciate.

This led me to think about how we can remedy the absence of nature at the Iowa State Fair and to an epiphany—as nature knows, I enjoy a good epiphany. Why not have a whole day of the Iowa State Fair dedicated to nature?! We already have Older Iowans' Day and the first Monday is always Veterans Day, and of course the omnipresent Iowa

Farm Bureau Federation has its own farmers day, but nothing about the land or nature. Just think of it, the county conservation boards could set up booths on the concourse describing their many parks and recreation facilities. The Conservation Districts of Iowa and its 99 soil and water conservation commissions could join in, describing all they do to protect the soil and water. For a day, the Iowa DNR could escape the confines of the brick nature temple at the entrance, the one with all the fish and furs, to tell the larger story of our state parks and all nature has to offer. The Iowa Sportsmen's Alliance would be there to feature its many members who enjoy hunting and fishing. The Audubon Society and all the other nature organizations would have displays and activities for folks of all ages. Jenni could bring her birds from Iowa Bird Rehabilitation and Marlene could come from the Iowa Wildlife Center. Ryan and the good folks at the Iowa Wildlife Federation would have stickers of critters for the kids and the Ikes would be there too! The Iowa Environmental Council could bring its coalition, and Practical Farmers of Iowa and the Iowa Farmers Union could explain the wonderful things they are doing to enhance nature and improve farming. The Iowa Natural Heritage Foundation and other land trusts could have booths to tell their stories featuring land projects and cooperating landowners from across the state.

Every spring the governor hosts a Gift to Iowa's Future Day honoring the landowners who have donated land to the public; in fact nature gives it a shout-out to conclude this chapter. The event is held in March at the State Capitol, but the ceremony could be moved to the fair to increase attendance. Consider holding it in the Livestock Pavilion before a crowd of hundreds just like the Governor's Charity Steer Show. We can let our imaginations run wild, inviting fairgoers to share their favorite links to nature and providing them with lists of ideas and activities to take home. Children could be engaged in celebrating nature and learning about how it enhances their lives. We could even arrange to have everyone who attends receive a free tree seedling or prairie plant to take home. What a wonderful idea if we all joined together to create Nature Day at our great Iowa State Fair!

## WHO PROTECTS NATURE?

Who do we expect to be the protectors of nature? If our only answer is public officials, then given the limited roles the Department of Natural Resources or the Environmental Protection Agency can play, we are going to be disappointed for many reasons. They may be understaffed or underfunded. They may be politically restrained. They may not have any legal authority to act, and they certainly can't be everywhere at once. Even if they do respond to a problem, for example, a river spill like the Nish, the process for enforcement is slow and fraught with dead ends.

The same can be said if we expect our laws and legal systems to be the protectors of nature. If we want the judges to do it, then first we have to have laws enacted giving them the authority. Those laws need to be applied by someone, and only then can the courts interpret them. The delays and dead ends in this process are real, as reflected in the Des Moines Water Works litigation and the Raccoon River public trust case. Having to resort to litigation is often a recipe for disappointment.

Can we expect the landowners, the people who actually own and control the land where nature exists, in a largely privately owned state like Iowa, to be the ones who will protect nature? This is possible and we have many examples, but it only occurs if they value it, respect it, or don't have more pressing, usually economic, reasons for not doing so. Does this leave members of the public—all of us—as the protectors? Yes, but we have only limited powers. For example, to act against others requires legal standing, especially if legal authority gives citizens a private right of action. This means the public is left in many ways to rely on politicians, and then the question becomes how to influence or educate them.

As a result, nature may not be particularly well protected because we haven't done a very good job preparing the foundation. We either outsource it to others or delegate it to those who may not care or may not have the authority to act. Then we are left to complain if they don't act. But doesn't this let us off the hook too easily? Isn't it all of our jobs, yours and mine, to be nature's protectors? Perhaps one reason we often fail is because we haven't spent time promoting the idea nature needs protecting or creating the tools and rewards for doing so. Perhaps we have left nature undefended thinking it doesn't need us to protect it, or it is someone else's job. Why not make it the job for all of us? Some groups are taking on this task. The Izaak Walton League of Iowa operates the "Save Our Streams" effort, the only national program that trains volunteers to protect waterways from pollution. Iowa once had the very popular IoWater citizen water monitoring program, and it could be revived. The point is—if we want to see nature defended, we need to roll up our sleeves and get to work, just like the person discussed next did in his lifetime.

## CREATING THE IOWA NATURE ADVOCATE: HONORING PAUL JOHNSON

How will we find the nature leaders to promote our vision and priorities? This issue has come into sharper focus in recent years in connection with the many developments discussed in chapter 9 on justice.

In the summer of 2021, the public trust doctrine was before the Iowa Supreme Court, and at the same time environmental groups had petitioned the director of the Department of Natural Resources to reverse the permit granted to the large cattle feedlot near Bloody Run Creek. It is no surprise the DNR director rejected the petition, saying she was powerless to review or reverse her staff's decision. Then, only a week later, Iowa's Supreme Court ruled 4-3 in the public trust doctrine case, saying the environmentalists lacked any standing to argue the state neglected its duty by failing to protect the Raccoon River. Unfortunately, by ruling this was a question for the legislature, the Court ducked the issue. The effect was to abandon its responsibility to uphold the constitutional idea the public trust doctrine gives citizens the right to expect shared natural resources, like our waters, are not left unprotected if public officials refuse to act.

The stories told in *Through Nature's Lens* show little has changed in Iowa's official view towards nature. Water withdrawals are approved, pipeline permits are granted, river pollution goes unpunished, and those responsible for protecting nature are left underfunded and unappreciated. These results make me think about how different things might be if a law passed by the Iowa legislature in 1989 had actually gone into effect. More importantly, they suggest it is not too late for us to act, to stand up—alongside nature—to ensure a healthy future for us all.

The 1989 law was authored by Representative Paul Johnson, a well-known environmental advocate and Leopoldian from the Decorah area. His idea was to create an independent state Office of the Environmental Advocate. The environmental advocate would serve as an intervener in legal proceedings to represent the interests of natural resources such as our soil, land, wildlife, and water. The law was one of the most original and progressive of its time in the nation, promoting the concept of the rights of nature. As a testament to Johnson's vision and his abilities as an advocate for nature, the bill passed both the Senate and the House and was sent on to the governor for signing.

Not surprisingly, the law was not well received by people who feared progress on environmental protections. As a result, the governor at that time, Terry Branstad, vetoed the law, saying it was unnecessary. He said Iowa's environmental laws were adequate to protect our soil and water, and our agencies could be trusted to do their jobs. In his view, the law presented a cops and robbers approach toward environmental protection, something Iowa did not need. What has happened in the years since shows how wrong he was about the adequacy of our laws and our willingness to enforce them. More importantly, events of recent years prove just how valuable such an office would have been to our state—and can still be today.

If Iowa had an environmental advocate, the office would no doubt have joined the public trust doctrine case and worked with the Department of Natural Resources to make sure that water-quality protections were enforced. Rather than leaving the protection of nature up to the voluntary desires of landowners, the advocate would have spoken for all who live along our rivers or have an interest in them. Similarly, the environmental advocate would have been there to speak on behalf of Bloody Run Creek. Instead, Iowa's leaders claimed to be powerless to act.

In an ironic twist, after leaving the Iowa legislature Paul Johnson served as director of the Iowa DNR and later as Chief of the USDA Natural Resources Conservation Service. It does not take wild speculation to know he would have demanded the DNR's staff review what many believed then and still today were egregious violations of administrative law in approving the cattle feedlot permit. You can be confident Johnson would be confronting Attorney General Bird for her failings on the Nish and urging the Iowa Supreme Court to act on behalf of the rivers.

Paul Johnson died in 2021, but he is not forgotten. *We Can Do Better: Collected Writings on Land, Conservation, and Public Policy*, a collection of his speeches and writings edited by Curt Meine, will be published in 2025. I wrote the following remembrance of Paul for the Iowa Natural Heritage Foundation in February 2021 at his passing:

> Iowa and the nation lost a towering figure in land conservation with the passing of Paul Johnson, a tree farmer, public official, state legislator and eloquent spokesman for nature. As you look across his long career in conservation it becomes evident he was the most significant voice for nature of our last half century. He leaves a legacy placing him squarely with others in the pantheon of Iowa's conservation leaders—Lacey, Wallace, Darling, and his hero, Aldo Leopold.
>
> I had the pleasure of knowing and working with Paul for forty years and always found him to be a soft spoken and gentle man, whose kindness cloaked an inner steel and fierce love for the natural world. Throughout his life in public service, on the farm and in his community of Decorah on the beautiful Upper Iowa River, Paul nurtured a love for the land and deep understanding of our responsibility to it. As a public servant he understood the value and power of using the law and our civic institutions to protect and enhance nature—the soil, land, water, and wildlife we all depend on to fulfill our lives. His career spanned many forms of public service—from serving as chief of the USDA Natural Resources Conservation

Service under President Clinton, to heading the Iowa Department of Natural Resources. But it was as a state legislator for several terms in the late '80s and early '90s where he left his most enduring contributions to our state. Two of his most important and lasting legislative accomplishments were passage of the Groundwater Protection Act of 1987 and creation of the Resource Enhancement and Protection Act (REAP).

REAP has dedicated close to $500 million dollars to state and local programs to protect natural lands, address conservation and water issues, and improve opportunities for Iowans to enjoy nature. Over 17,000 local projects in every corner and county of the state have benefited from REAP, and it continues to be the state's single most important source of funding for local conservation initiatives and innovations.

The Groundwater Protection Act is responsible for many improvements including the closure of the over 1,000 agricultural drainage wells sending surface pollution directly into our aquifers. Paul was a humble man who would be quick to point out these legislative achievements were not his alone but took a team of forward looking Iowa leaders.

The Groundwater Protection Act is perhaps most widely known for creating the Leopold Center for Sustainable Agriculture housed at Iowa State University. The Center—which Paul specifically named for Iowa's greatest conservation visionary—was guided by a citizen advisory board and funded with a small tax on nitrogen fertilizers, pesticide registration fees and periodic general appropriations. During its 30 years of active operation, the Center funded hundreds of innovative research projects which helped provide a national model for sustainable agriculture and the scientific basis for many of the soil conservation and water quality practices being promoted today. Unfortunately, a short-sighted legislative decision several years ago has essentially ended the work of the Center. This decision illustrated something Paul and Leopold both knew only too well. Our efforts to protect nature must be vigilant because the powerful political forces that see land only in economic terms fear any effort to prioritize conservation.

The legacy Paul Johnson left us is one we should value and protect. He was a Leopoldian in the truest sense, and in my work I often looked to him for inspiration and wisdom. I valued his honesty and commitment to public service, the land and our state. He had a calming demeanor and you felt you were in the presence of a person with great wisdom and sensitivity. When he spoke in public you knew people were listening with special attention because his comments were not idle filler but instead were thoughtful and heartfelt. He wasn't one for the feel good double speak some officials seem to excel in, instead he spoke with candor and honesty about our challenges in protecting soil and water and our need to do better.

Even with setbacks, Paul did not get discouraged in his work. He was a beacon who encouraged leaders to do more, educated landowners about their opportunities, and inspired organizations like the INHF to continue to expand our efforts. Yes, Iowa has lost a champion for our land and nature, woods and wildlife, but Paul Johnson's work and his spirit live on in the land and in our hearts. He left a legacy and foundation on which we must build.

I can think of no better tribute the friends of nature and the state of Iowa can give Paul than to enact a modern version of his environmental advocate proposal, creating a permanent legal authority to ensure the tools of justice can be used on behalf of nature. Your reaction might be—are you kidding, how could such a law survive given our current political climate! Paul, like Nature, took the long view. Good ideas—like nature—are resilient. We might not enact such a law this year or in ten years—but this does not mean the idea and the ideal are not worth our efforts. We owe it to nature and to Paul to continue trying.

## Are You Listening Now?

The professor is nearing the end and trying to wrap this up but I have one more matter to discuss. My question is - are you finally going to get serious about addressing your water quality issue? In June, 2025 the Central Iowa Water Works imposed a ban on lawn watering for its 600,000 customers but the reason wasn't due to a drought. The reason was because the Raccoon and Des Moines river water was so polluted with nitrates coming from farm fields CIWW couldn't obtain or produce enough "clean" water to blend with the river sources to get the drinking water it was to provide its customers below the 10 mg/L legal threshold. This meant they had to take the unprecedented step of banning lawn watering to "preserve" the supply of clean water. The episode provided rich fodder for every news channel and reporter, to ask why are the rivers so contaminated? It even led the Des Moines Register to ask if it is time to rethink Iowa's reliance on voluntary only approaches for "encouraging" farmers to reduce fertilizer use and to adopt farming practices limiting the loss of excessive nitrates. As fate has it, this farm fueled water "crisis" coincided with the Polk County Supervisors deciding whether to release a comprehensive source water study completed in March. The 18 month study, launched using American Rescue Plan funding, was conducted by a team of 16 well regarded scientists who examined available data and studies. Wouldn't you know it, when public pressure led to the report finally being released, their findings concluded over 80% of the contamination problems plaguing the water supply come from agriculture. As you can only imagine this episode sent the farm groups and Iowa politicans scurrying to fire up their excuse generators to explain why this is really not their fault, how it is unfair to point fingers at agriculture, and to remind the public how important corn and ethanol are to the state. It is too early to predict where this is all going to lead but you won't be surprised to know I find it a hopeful development in your struggle to protect our waters. When added to your cancer worries the weight of public opinion could be shifting.

## WHAT DO IOWANS WANT FOR NATURE?
## TWELVE IDEAS TO CONSIDER

We have traveled many miles using nature's lens to think about our future. Our discussion has covered a broad array of issues with a common touchstone: nature. It is not my job to be the official spokesman for nature in our state. No one can assume that role. The good news is we have legions of citizens filling that role in every county and every corner. Having met many of them at the summits and in my earlier books I can summarize their hopes for nature. Here are twelve ideas to consider about what Iowans want for nature. See if you agree.

1) You want it to thrive—to provide an outlet for nature-based activities and, conversely, you don't want to see it diminished or abused.

2) You want more of it, as reflected in your support for IWILL, for local bond efforts like those in Story and Johnson counties, for your membership in organizations like Iowa Natural Heritage Foundation. Iowans want more open spaces, larger parks, longer trails, and more access to nearby nature.

3) You want public officials to tackle water-quality problems. You want an end to the delays, excuses and deference to agriculture. You want leaders to lead and to explain why water quality is either not a

priority or to do something about it.

4) You want to elevate the recognition of nature issues in policy debates so what landowners want and the "no role for regulation" mantra do not control all decisions. You want officials to give more weight and value to nature, to recognize its loss can be permanent.

5) You want more balance in policy actions and want nature to be heard, respected, and valued, not considered an afterthought or a luxury. You want nature to be included in discussions, meaning those who speak for it, not just those who want to harness it, will be included.

6) You want nature to be recognized as a public good and a public right. The debate about nature is like the debate about funding public schools, its existence and access are public rights not to be sacrificed for private desires.

7) You want public officials to do their jobs, to protect the public interest not just make life safer for polluters or private actors. The same is true for lawmakers and judges.

8) You want nature to contribute to your health, not be a threat with unsafe water, increasing cancer rates, poor air quality, and mental health worries. You see nature as a positive health benefit along with healthful food and wellness.

9) You want a piece of nature, a place to call your own. It may be private, such as a lake house, or it may be public, a place you frequent like a favorite hiking trail or beach. You see nature as a place to leave your mark in a positive way such as restoring a prairie or an oak savanna.

10) You want to interact with nature, not just see it in the abstract. You want to be immersed in it, to hike, swim, boat, fish, hunt, bike, birdwatch, and all the other ways of engaging with nature. Iowans want to feel the sun and wind and enjoy the peace, quiet, and beauty

of being in nature.

11) You want to add to nature, to improve it, and to ensure it has a future. You see nature not as something to take but as a place to give back to, to restore and protect.

12) You want nature to be shared and passed on. Solitude, peace, and enjoyment are valuable, but so is sharing nature with family and friends. You want the next generation to be educated so they love nature and can carry on the work that guarantees its future.

## TAKING THE NATURE PLEDGE

When creating the Iowa Nature Summits, one of my intentions was to craft a Nature Pledge—a straightforward, concise statement of nature principles for attendees and organizations. I share it with you as something to consider.

1) I will advocate for steady growth in funding from all sources— federal, state, county, local, and private—to adequately protect Iowa's natural resources, including employing the staff needed to maintain and protect them, to ensure the public has the opportunity and ability to enjoy nature in all its forms.

2) I will work to expand opportunities for all citizens to enjoy the outdoors, to engage with nature whether on waterways, or in county and state parks and wildlife management areas, both on public land and on private land whose owners have voluntarily made accessible to the public through easements and other arrangements.

3) I will support actions to protect water quality, soil health, prairies, forests, open spaces, wildlife populations, and other features of a healthy natural environment from actions unwisely wasting, degrading, or damaging these vital natural features, and I will work to enforce

needed public safeguards.

4) I will promote educational programs, private collaborations, and public actions so all Iowans understand their personal role and responsibility in protecting nature and its resources.

5) I will encourage efforts to ensure public officials at all levels understand the vital role of the natural environment and the contributions it provides to our economy, public health, and quality of life and encourage them to consider nature in the performance of their official responsibilities.

## Two Great Days for Nature with More to Come

Well, you've made it to the end. The professor has taken us on quite a journey, with many high points and some low ones too, especially now with your uncertain political times. It has been a pleasure to chime in with color commentary, in particular, when there is good news to share. This is how I want to leave you—with a sense of hope and opportunity. I found both on two days in March, 2025 in events taking place at the Iowa State Capitol. Yes, I was surprised, too! The two days were Gift to Iowa's Future Day on March 13 and Celebrate Iowa's Outdoors Day a week later on March 20. Both days showcased what Iowans are doing to support nature—me—and showed their love for the outdoors (also me!).

The Gift to Iowa's Future Day honors Iowans who have made permanent donations of land to the state or county. It recognizes how their decisions to convert family lands into public lands will benefit all of you. The day featured two dozen landowners whose generous actions added hundreds of acres of unique Iowa natural lands from across my breadth—wetlands to timber, prairie to river corridors—to the public. The Iowa Natural Heritage Foundation held a luncheon before the event at the capitol to recognize the more than one dozen families whose gifts of land were facilitated by working with foundation staff. Their donations involved a wide range of legal tools from outright gifts to bargain sales, and conservation easements and reserved life estates, showing how flexible the technologies of justice can be to support me.

Celebrate Iowa's Outdoors Day was a new venture, the brainchild of Anna Gray, policy director for the Iowa Natural Heritage Foundation. She is another of the professor's former students, one he is very proud to claim. Her idea was to gather in the statehouse rotunda the broad array of Iowa nature organizations and interested citizens to share their message of love and respect for me with Iowa lawmakers and to celebrate their common work. The event has a parallel to the gatherings at the Iowa Nature Summits but was intentionally aimed at a larger audience of lawmakers, media, and the public. The day was a resounding success with over 50 organizations joining to sponsor and display their work. Hundreds of citizens attended, all brought together to honor me—and to enjoy a delicious free breakfast. It was the first day of spring and I tried to help by delivering a sunny blue sky day to enliven the activities. It was much appreciated after the surprise blizzard I had unloaded the day before—sorry about that, I just needed to clear one more piece of winter out of inventory!

I highlight these two days in closing because they illustrate the good things you do and because they give me hope. Even with your politics, the turmoil and upheavals, the delays in acting when the needed path forward seems clear, there is still reason for hope. I have told you many times nature takes the long look, and I am patient. Days like these help restore my faith in you, leaving me optimistic, more confident, and more hopeful your work will be rewarded. Keep up the fight, love and honor me, and don't lose sight of your dreams for a healthier and more beautiful natural state.

# ACKNOWLEDGEMENTS

The words are all mine but many hands and minds were involved in helping shape them. I must begin by thanking Steve Semken of Ice Cube Press for making all of my three nature books possible and for his trust in the value of letting me speak my mind for Iowa's land, water, and wildlife. A special thank you to Holly Carver for her editing skills and for making this book much brighter and readable. My friend Pat Boddy also gave the draft a thorough edit making many helpful comments. The Iowa Nature Summits are discussed in several places and my planning team all helped shaped the ideas reflected here: Joe McGovern, Christine Curry, Pat Boddy (again!), Ryan Smith, Dr. Richard Deming, and Jennifer Zwagerman. All the many individuals and organizations who have sponsored the Iowa Nature Summits helped make this book possible, especially my friend Amy Goldman Fowler and the Lillian Goldman Charitable Trust. Many Iowans are doing their part for nature – the friends of nature protecting land; the individuals recognized as Iowa Nature Champions; and the board, staff, and members of the Iowa Natural Heritage Foundation all deserve thanks for their work on behalf of Iowa. The two dozen friends who gather for our weekly SPARKS calls will recognize many of these themes and can take pride in having helped shape them. I appreciate the contributions of the Drake University Law School, my professional home now for over 40 years, for providing not just an office and brilliant colleagues but also for the intellectual freedom and opportunity to share truths I believe need shared about our state. Thank you to the many readers of *The Land Remains* and *The River Knows*, who encouraged me to keep writing, to add this one more voice to the chorus. Of course I thank my bride, Khanh, who makes a few reluctant appearances herein, for making our home at Sunstead the beautiful and nourishing place it is.

As a final note, I would be remiss for failing to honor the beauty of our state and all nature has offered us to enjoy. From the scenic vistas of the Sylvan Runkel Preserve in the northwest, to the flowing river in the Lacey Keosaqua State Park in the southeast, from the beautiful bluff top of Capoli in the northeast, to the open skies of Waubonsie State Park and the Loess Hills in the southwest, our Iowa contains countless examples of nature's bounty. These are natural gifts where we can find hope and inspiration even in these trying times. Remember nature is patient and takes the long look – good advice for us all.

# Reading List from *Through Nature's Lens*

Andrew Bacevich, *Age of Illusions: How America Squandered its Cold War Victory*

Dan Barry, *The Boys in the Bunkhouse: Servitude and Salvation in the Heartland*

Frank Bruni, *The Age of Grievance*

Rachel Carson, *Silent Spring*

Ron Chernow, *Alexander Hamilton*

William O Douglas, *Go East, Young Man*

Kristin Kobes Du Mez, *Jesus and John Wayne: How White Evangelicals Corrupted a Faith and Fractured a Nation*

Dan Egan, *The Devil's Element: Phosphorus and a World Out of Balance*

Stephen Fox, *The American Conservation Movement: John Muir and His Legacy*

Ian Frazier, *Paradise Bronx: the Life and Times of New York's Greatest Borough*

Neil D. Hamilton, *The Land Remains*

Neil D. Hamilton, *The River Knows*

Kirke Wallace Johnson, *The Feather Thief: Beauty, Obsession, and the Natural History Heist of the Century*

Steve Johnson, *World In Their Hands: Original Thinkers, Doers, Fighters and the Future of Conservation*

Chris Jones, *The Swine Republic: Struggles with the Truth about Agriculture and Water Quality*

Ezra Klein and Derek Thompson, *Abundance*

Aldo Leopold, *A Sand County Almanac*

Richard Louv, *Last Child in the Woods*

Richard Louv, *The Nature Principal*

M. Margaret McKeown, *Citizen Justice: the Environmental Legacy of William O Douglas, Public Advocate and Conservation Champion*

Curt Meine, ed., *We Can Do Better: Collected Writings on Land, Conservation, and Public Policy, Speeches and writings of Paul Johnson*

Douglas Monk, *On the Trail of Lyman Dillon*

Leila Philip, *Beaverland: How One Weird Rodent Made America*

Pope Francis, *Encyclical Letter, Laudato Si'*

Jedediah Purdy, *After Nature: a Politics of the Anthropocene*

Douglas Tallamy, *Nature's Best Hope*

Dyan Zaslowsky, *Rosalie Edge, Hawk of Mercy: The Activist Who Saved Nature from the Conservationists*

# INDEX

about publisher here